"In a post-Christendom era, a primer Sunquist offers us a book that is fluent and fresh, combining profundity and down-to-earth simplicity, with healthy doses of humor and no-nonsense realism. After reading it, you are very likely to agree with him when he writes: 'the church is really one of God's best ideas.'"

Jeremy Begbie, Thomas A. Langford Distinguished Professor of Theology, Duke University

"Rising generations who wonder about the church's significance today will find *Why Church?* a compelling and timely book. Scott Sunquist masterfully weaves together clear theological claims with his own experiences along with beautiful illustrations of the global church. Taking on the real challenges we face to live like one body, this book will heighten your imagination by breaking down predominant conceptions of the church as a sterile religious institution. Sunquist increased my curiosity to once again examine the movement from worship to witness as well as the critical nature of our shared Christian identity. As you read, you will experience being invited to come and kneel with communities who are on the go."

Sharon Galgay Ketcham, author of *Reciprocal Church*, professor of theology and ministry at Gordon College, MA

"In this deceptively profound book, Scott Sunquist writes, 'the church was Jesus' idea.' Local congregations have two grand purposes: to worship and do mission. Utilizing two millennia of church life and contemporary stories from around the world, he weaves a wonderful tapestry of biblical teaching and personal illustration. Only a personally pious and missional historian could write such a book."

Alec Hill, president emeritus, InterVarsity Christian Fellowship

"In *Why Church?* Scott Sunquist brings clarity and power to who and what we are as the church of Jesus. As a seminary colleague, I appreciate the way Sunquist brings a wealth of history and research to our current context. As a pastor, I am strengthened by the way he investigates contemporary expressions of the church around the world and then focuses on what it means for us to help our folks deeply engage the two biblical reasons for the church (*worship* and *mission*). As a friend, I am grateful that Scott has given the church an essential reminder of our call as believers. Every pastor, staff person, and leader needs to use *Why Church?* as a resource for taking us to new heights as leaders of the Lord's household."

Chap Clark, pastor, St. Andrew's Presbyterian Church, formerly vice provost, Fuller Theological Seminary

"In a day and age when people say, 'I love Jesus, but I can do without the church,' Scott Sunquist reveals the error of such thinking. You cannot get Jesus without his church. It is his body and bride. With the mind of a scholar, the passion of a missionary, and the heart of a pastor, Scott provides both a correction and a call to return to the sense and sensibilities of the initial followers of Jesus who turned the world upside down."

Claude Alexander, bishop, The Park Church, Charlotte, NC

SCOTT W. SUNQUIST

WHY CHURCH?

A Basic Introduction

Foreword by Richard J. Mouw

Academic

An imprint of InterVarsity Press
Downers Grove, Illinois

InterVarsity Press
P.O. Box 1400, Downers Grove, IL 60515-1426
ivpress.com
email@ivpress.com

InterVarsity Press® is the book-publishing division of InterVarsity Christian Fellowship/USA®, a movement of
students and faculty active on campus at hundreds of universities, colleges, and schools of nursing in the United
States of America, and a member movement of the International Fellowship of Evangelical Students. For
information about local and regional activities, visit intervarsity.org.

While any stories in this book are true, some names and identifying information may have been changed to protect
the privacy of individuals.

Cover design: Faceout Studio
Interior design: Daniel van Loon

ISBN 978-0-8308-5238-3 (print)
ISBN 978-0-8308-7235-0 (digital)

Printed in the United States of America ♾

Library of Congress Cataloging-in-Publication Data
Names: Sunquist, Scott W. (Scott William), 1953- author.
Title: Why church? : a basic introduction / Scott W. Sunquist.
Description: Downers Grove, IL : IVP Academic, [2019] | Includes bibliographical references and index.
Identifiers: LCCN 2019013106 (print) | LCCN 2019015972 (ebook) | ISBN 9780830872350 (eBook) | ISBN
    9780830852383 (pbk. : alk. paper) | ISBN 9780830872350 (ebk.)
Subjects: LCSH: Church. | Public worship.
Classification: LCC BV600.3 (ebook) | LCC BV600.3 .S86 2019 (print) | DDC 262—dc23
LC record available at https://lccn.loc.gov/2019013106

P   25   24   23   22   21   20   19   18   17   16   15   14   13   12   11   10   9   8   7   6   5   4   3   2   1

Y   37   36   35   34   33   32   31   30   29   28   27   26   25   24   23   22   21   20   19

This book is dedicated to the next generation of those in

*"the household of God, which is the church of the
living God, the pillar and bulwark of the truth."*
1 Timothy 3:15 NRSV

This is also dedicated to the generation after that.

*Thus, I would like to dedicate this to our four children (and their
spouses) and our grandchildren (who number ten so far).
May they derive the same joy we have received and continue
to receive from being part of the body of Christ.*

Caroline Noel (Sunquist) and Timothy Joseph Becker†
Luke Allen, Samuel William, and Hosanna Noel

Bethany Susan (Sunquist) and Joshua Thomas Lomelino
Isaiah Thomas, Eliana Jane, Gloria Grace, and Lucia Pearl

Elisha Stephen and Tara Ashley Sunquist
Rooney Emerson

Jesse Scott and Christy Anna Sunquist
June Eileen and Ove Boone

His intent was that now, through the church, the
manifold wisdom of God should be made known to
the rulers and authorities in the heavenly realms.

EPHESIANS 3:10

CONTENTS

FOREWORD

Richard J. Mouw

WRITING A FOREWORD TO SOMEONE else's book is a unique assignment. It is certainly different from a book review. Reviewers are expected to offer some criticisms. It's okay to say in a review, for example, that you wish the author had said more about so-and-so, and an honest book review will even on occasion lodge some serious objections to some things that appear in the book. But doing that in a foreword would be a betrayal of the point of the assignment, instead communicating, "Think twice before reading on!"

I have never written a foreword where I have felt the need to lodge some criticisms about what was in the book. On a couple of occasions I have covered myself on a point or two by including this sort of clause: "While not every reader will agree with everything the author says in these pages, nevertheless . . ." But my "nevertheless" has signaled my encouragement to the reader to keep turning the pages.

I don't even have a qualifying clause to offer here. I agreed to write the foreword before reading what Scott Sunquist had written, not only because he is my friend but because he is a friend from whom I have learned much. I had no worries that I would dislike the views he would be setting forth.

Even if I did have some minor disagreements along the way—which I did not—Scott made it easy for me when he wrote in the early pages that "this book will irritate most people a little and (hopefully) encourage them a lot." It was good to know that he would not feel betrayed if I happened to find something irritating in the book.

The irritation never happened, though. I like this book a lot, and he clarified some issues for me theologically. I have a strong scholarly interest in topics relating to church, and Scott offers many creative insights into topics I think much about these days: diversity in worship styles, crosscultural dimensions, the role of the church in the larger narrative of God's redeeming and renewing purposes, the public role(s) of the Christian community. On all of these subjects and many others, he provides perspectives that are informative and compelling.

I also like the way he weaves insights about his own personal journey into the discussion. Many of us in the theological world pay considerable attention these days to cultural context, but we often do not attend to the very personal contexts that inform our scholarly discussions of a theological topic. Scott tells us, for example, about how he drifted away from church in his teenage years because much of what he experienced in worship had no connection to his adolescent preoccupations. He confesses that much of this was due to his own cluelessness about spiritual matters—which is a welcome dose of candor. But his teenage experience also clearly shapes the direction that much of his subsequent theological reflection has taken on what it means to be "church."

Scott says in that early comment that he wants to *encourage* us in our efforts to get clearer about the nature and mission of the church, and he more than fulfills that intention in what he has written here. I am grateful for that, because we really need what he has to teach us. The case set forth in these pages is not only profoundly biblical, but it is compelling in the wisdom that it offers for our ongoing efforts to be a people who love and serve the cause of the gospel.

In short, what the reader will discover in these pages is a delightful and stimulating blend of personal disclosure, solid theology, global savvy, and creative counsel for what it means to be a people who are attempting to be faithful to the call to participate in God's mission in the world. Read on in confidence!

ACKNOWLEDGMENTS

I WOULD LIKE TO THANK the following people for taking the time to read over all or parts of this volume, giving very helpful feedback along the way. I avoided many errors by learning from their comments and questions. The following people represent many different church traditions, levels of education, and experience in the church. I am sure none agree with everything in here, but it is a better volume because they took the time to read and comment. I believe that the final product (which you now hold) is more meaningful, winsome, and accurate. Please don't blame them for what you find irritating in the book, but thank them for making it better. As you will see, we have some relatives and friends, some seminary and college folks, but also some global friends whose churches look very different from ours. I appreciate every one of them and am very thankful for their help.

Nancy S. Sunquist

Jesse S. Sunquist

Elisha S. Sunquist

Juan Martínez

Dwight Radcliffe

Robert Solomon

Charlie Cotherman

Michael Gilton

Paul Kemeny

Kevin Henson

Len Tang

Chris Thomas

Elizabeth Trexler

Tom Pappalardo
Jen Graffius
Sharon Ketcham
Max and Jasmine Boyle
Mike Moore
Don Dawson
Roberta King
Sue Ramsey

A special thanks goes to Gwen McWhorter, who took many of the comments from the above readers and summarized them for me, made the corrections I should have made, and made some very helpful suggestions.

My first-line editor throughout the process was my wife, Nancy. She appears by name in the book, and her handiwork and good eye permeates the book. We have had some delightful conversations about the Church through the years. Thank you, again. We make a good team.

1

CHURCH

Only Two Purposes

A LITTLE CHURCH EXERCISE

When my wife and I moved from western Pennsylvania to Southern California, we visited a lot of churches that first year. Actually, we visited about thirty-five churches—about thirty more than my wife wanted to visit. We learned a lot about what it means to be a church from visiting so many and such different churches, even though we were only visiting on Sunday mornings. We visited new churches being planted that had an attendance from about twenty people to a couple thousand. Most of these new churches had no denominational affiliation. We visited Lutheran, Roman Catholic, Presbyterian, Covenant, Bible, Orthodox, and Baptist churches. We visited churches that were mostly white (one) and mostly African American, Thai, Chinese, Korean, Hispanic, and of course, a lot of multicultural churches. (Spanish is the most common language of Los Angeles County we discovered.) We learned a lot about worship, hospitality, identity, conventions of behavior, and liturgy.

Another small thing we learned is about when people arrive at worship and when they leave. Patterns of attendance (when you come and when you leave) express something about what you value in worship. Some people want to miss the offering; others want to come only for the sermon. Below I present some patterns we observed, and later in the volume I will draw some comparisons with many African indigenous churches and Chinese churches. Read these three paragraphs below and then think about what each paragraph tells us about what the congregation values in worship.

Roman Catholic worship. We arrived at church almost exactly on time, and there was still a lot of milling around the sanctuary. By the time of the procession with the Bible and cross being carried down the aisle, most of the pews were filled. It was a very diverse crowd: all ages and ethnic backgrounds. Toward the end of the service was the Eucharist.[1] People would come down the center aisle and return to their seats down the side—wait, did I say *return*? Actually, about half of the people did not return to their seats. They came down the center aisle, received the wafer and wine, and exited stage right. There was still another hymn, more prayer, some announcements, another prayer and then the benediction. But the church was about half full when all this was wrapping up.

African American church. The service was longer than most of the churches we attended. Unlike the Roman Catholic Church people were not "on time." Most of the congregation did not arrive until about half an hour into the two-and-a-half-hour service. People kept coming in during the hymns, some special music selections, opening prayers, a small pre-sermon sermon, and prayers for couples and their marriages. By the time we got to the sermon (an hour or so into the service) the church was very full. The sermon was more of a community experience than in most churches; people shouted approval or concern as the preacher delivered his message. People stayed until the end, but most people do not know how the worship begins. Most arrive on the train as it is moving, so to speak.

New church plant. A number of newer churches, related to no denominations, but often in semiformal association with church planting networks, followed this pattern. Large numbers of people mill around outside before the service starts. In fact, a large number stand outside drinking coffee even after the worship starts. Worship starts with a brief introduction, a story, and/or a prayer. The meeting place has few if any religious symbols. In every way imaginable, the atmosphere is informal. People stand to sing worship songs for twenty to forty minutes. After about half of the singing is done (whether it is twenty or forty minutes, they seem to have a feel for the right timing) the congregation fills up. People seem to enjoy the worship music, and it is usually very well done, but about half of the congregations miss half of the worship music. After the praise music the other elements happen very fast: offering, Communion (infrequently), prayer (brief), the main message, song, and exit. People stay until the very end and usually stay around to talk and drink more coffee.

WHAT IS IN A NAME?

You can tell a lot about a person by their name. Scott may be from Scotland (or a distant relative was from there). Joshua was probably born after 1975—or during biblical times. Harmony's parents may have been hippies in the late 1960s. Jesus is either Latin American (possibly a baseball player) or an important person in the Bible.

Sometimes you can tell a lot about a church by its name. John Calvin Presbyterian Church says it all. This is a church that follows the teachings of John Calvin, one of the great leaders of the Reformation. First Baptist is a church that does not baptize infants, and it was established before Second Baptist. Then there is St. Sergius or St. Nicholas; they are most likely Orthodox churches that follow an ancient liturgy from the third and fourth centuries in the Mediterranean world. John Wesley is probably a Methodist church, and St. Thomas or Sts. Peter and Paul are very likely Roman Catholic churches.

If we know a little history we can usually tell something about a church before we step in the front door (the entry hall, often called the narthex). However, I have visited a lot of churches recently—and spoken at a few of them—and it is much harder to figure out what church names mean for these newer churches. Here are a few that I know about personally:

- Reality, LA
- Upper Room
- Epicentre
- New City Church
- Open Door
- House of Manna
- Hillsong
- Mosaic
- Dream Center
- Harvest Rock Church
- Prism Church

Church names are significant in other areas of the world as well. Some newer churches in Nigeria have unusual sounding names, but often the

name says something that makes us want to poke our heads inside. Here
are a few of the more dramatic names of churches in the largest country
in Africa:

- Guided Missiles Church
- Hurricane Miracle Ministry
- Healing Tsunami Ministry
- Satan in Trouble Ministry
- Fire for Fire Ministry
- Run for Your Life Ministry
- The Yoke Must Broke Ministry
- OPM—Other People's Money
- Strong Hand of God Ministry

So what is in a name? A church name, like a personal name, expresses
something of the identity of the church. Earlier churches that have long-
standing traditions look back to their founding or what it was that gave
them meaning as they looked around them (Lutheran means we are not
Catholic; Mennonite means we follow Menno Simons, a sixteenth-
century reformer). Today, newer churches choose names according to
what they want to express about their understanding of what it means to
be the church. We have a church named Open Door, which is a place that
welcomes all people. A church that is a new expression of the Church in
the city is called New City Church. Or, for many churches in Nigeria, we
experience God's power and invite others to experience that same power
(Hurricane Miracles). All this raises an important question today:
a question more basic than asking what a name tells us.

WHAT IS THE CHURCH?

Is a church just something we create to serve our purposes, or to serve
God's purposes, as we understand them? Is a church merely an expression
of an old tradition that we hold on to as a way of maintaining an old
tradition? Or is the church something more vital, more meaningful,
dynamic, or important than just maintaining a (largely) meaningless
institutional practice? Is the Church really the body of Christ? I capi-
talized *Church* just now because, with an uppercase *C*, it refers to the
universal church, that is, all churches throughout the world and
throughout time. Spelled with a lowercase *c*, *church* refers to a local
church or a particular part or expression of the Church. So is the Church

really God's only plan for the redemption of the world? This seems hard to believe when we look at what happens at any one local church. Not all churches look or act like Jesus in the world. Many churches in the West are slowly (or even quickly) dying. How are these churches pointing us to Jesus?

I remember attending worship at the age of thirteen, a period of time when I was searching for my identity in the midst of the confusion and excitement of adolescence. I remember thinking, or rather beginning to decide, that church (certainly worship) was pretty strange and irrelevant to me. In my teen years we attended a wealthy suburban church in the northeast. The pastor drove a memorable yellow Cadillac Coupe de Ville. To our all-white suburban church he preached about civil rights, poverty, and our responsibility to the homeless. I went to a Sunday school class and remember watching a boy steal a girl's purse during a prayer. I know, my eyes should have been closed, but I was an adolescent. I knew almost nothing about the Bible, and I found the denominational lessons both childish and rather odd. Maybe it was just me, but Moses, Jesus, Martin Luther, John Knox, and John Calvin all seemed like mythical figures to me, of the same type as Superman, Batman, Paul Bunyan, or Gandalf.

Of course, I was an adolescent, but still, it all seemed strange to my young teen ears and eyes. In fact as I look back now it still seems rather strange and irrelevant, if not irreverent. I didn't understand the language that seemed to be an insider lingo: the *Gloria Patri*, the narthex, the Creed, confession, even pulpit and sanctuary! When I joined the church I was really learning a foreign language, a strange culture, as I was taught what all this (apparently) meaningless stuff meant. I was being enculturated *into* church culture and *out of* my local public junior high culture. Church was a whole separate existence from my week of playing soccer, studying for exams, learning to negotiate adolescent life, deciding what group to eat with at school lunch, and watching TV.

And yet, there was something that kept me from straying too far from my church families, friends, and activities. These people had some different values and habits, some of which were inviting, even intriguing. We went on retreats with the youth, and we were not expected (or allowed) to get drunk and act stupid (maybe a little stupid). Families came together, and I saw many more fathers present than I did in the broader culture, fathers who were present with their families. There was something oddly attractive about the mystery and holy silence during a worship service. We would have a time to silently confess our personal sins. I didn't think that was really all that odd because I knew I was a sinner. I felt bad about many of my thoughts and found it pleasant that I could talk to someone (God) about it. The church was one place where older people knew my name and spoke to me. That also did not happen in the broader culture. So even as I drew away from church, I felt an attraction to this institution, or this special community, that I didn't wholly understand.

So I was intrigued by this strangeness of church, but slowly I drifted away to a life that seemed more meaningful to me. I suspect that this is the experience of many young people and young adults too. Does church need to be so foreign and odd compared to our other six days of existence each week? Yes and no. What is the purpose of the Church and of any local church? Can it (should it) be more meaningful and still profound and mysterious?

CHURCH: HISTORY AND CULTURE, SPEAK TO ME!

Many years have passed since I had my crisis of church faith. My conversion to Jesus at the age of sixteen was in some ways a conversion away from the church I had come to experience and only partially love. I had tried to leave the church and just focus on Christian friends and relatives, but I kept getting drawn back. I have, frankly, attended churches that have been frustrating and even embarrassing when I have brought my friends. I have been to churches that support abortion (which I do not) and churches that really don't want to be multicultural (which I do want). I have attended churches that talk about the Bible, but really do not study it, and I have attended churches that talk about love and diversity, but seem only welcoming to older white liberals. I have also been to churches where you have to know how and when to turn pages in a liturgy book and when to stand up, speak, be silent, or sit down—things I didn't know and so found frustrating.

With all of these frustrations and imperfections in churches, I have come to realize that I am really the main problem. At the same time I have discovered that the Church is really one of God's best ideas (second only to Jesus). Two issues regarding the Church have helped me come to these conclusions. First is history. As I was traveling through life, trying to be faithful to Jesus as a university student, then as a junior high teacher/soccer coach, then as an InterVarsity staff worker, then as a missionary, and now as a seminary professor, I found out that I had become a historian. I have now written a lot about history, mostly about the history of the church. I have discovered that the Church and local churches are amazing, diverse, complex, and very, very meaningful. I have found that many governments find the church their greatest enemy! They try to crush the church because it threatens their rule.

My frustration and even anger at the church decades ago was in part because of my ignorance of what the church is. Was I to blame? Partly, but my fairly liberal mainline "Christendom"[2] church was also to blame. I was involved in a local community that was much more beautiful and much more profound than I was led to believe. If I had known about the early church, living in the shadow of Jesus, the former dead person, I think I would have been much more committed to the idea of church. If I had known about how early Christians developed patterns of living and dying in imitation of Jesus, it would have helped me a great deal. Since that time I have come to have deep respect for the great martyrs of the church—those who died for their faith, refusing to recant or deny Jesus as Lord—missionaries, and even some pastors and priests (people I had no desire to emulate until I met some great ones). For me, history has revealed the richness, diversity, and even the joy of church. I plan to talk a lot about history in the following pages, mostly about people in history, which is far more interesting than facts and dates. But I will also talk about the church around the world. Thus, we will try to understand the church through time and throughout the world.

Related to history is culture. I have discovered that the Church, or at least any local church, is embedded in local communities and larger societies. Churches are so different from one another! Some churches have incense and bells, large statues and paintings and stained glass; others have dirt floors and split cane walls. Some churches have no music, and others thrive on worship that is mostly singing and chanting. I have been to churches with joy and dancing (even dancing when the people come up to give their offerings), and I have been to very solemn churches where I have struggled to follow the little book in the pew with bold type and normal type and seasonal prayers that make it very difficult for the outsider to follow. At times I wish all these different churches were more similar, and then I catch myself: how wonderful it is that churches reflect different cultures and even different issues and themes from the Bible.

> The best of churches, I believe, are both connected to the past and culturally relevant: *connected* and *contextual.*

The best of churches, I believe, are both connected to the past and culturally relevant: *connected* and *contextual.* They are mysteriously ancient, and they make sense to the local visitor. I hope that after a few hours of reading this book you will come to a similar conclusion for yourself.

CHURCH HAS ONLY TWO PURPOSES

I think it is helpful to rethink what church is by reflecting on the two basic purposes of the church. I wish someone had told me this when I was younger, at a time when I was wondering what the church was all about. When we understand the purpose of an elementary school, then the architecture, programs, types of people hired, and schedule all make sense. Likewise, when we find out the purpose of a local police station, the various activities and regulations (and the bars on the windows) all begin to make sense. The same can be said of the purpose and design of a bathroom, coffee shop, or a racetrack.

We cannot understand the purpose of the church just by looking at our local church or looking at why churches split during the Reformation.

We need to go back to the source and ask the question, What was Jesus' intent in gathering disciples around him? Even more to the point, What was Jesus' intent as he spoke to his followers in those last days before he departed this earth? Then, would Jesus recognize the church today as what he intended?

Jesus came to start a movement, a small movement of marginal Jewish men and women who were from western Asia. He called it yeast: just a little bit can change the whole lump (Mt 13:33). Jesus wanted them to continue what he started, to bring about just and compassionate change beginning with individuals. Scripture tells us that he intended for this movement to extend to the farthest and most remote corners of the earth and become the most diverse and inclusive movement the world has known. It happened. Jesus intended to initiate, through apparent defeat (dying on the cross), a movement that would conquer death, injustice, and even disease, extending what he called "the kingdom of God." He said it would be like yeast in dough or like a tiny mustard seed that becomes a great tree. As I mentioned above, this is God's only plan for redeeming all of humanity, all societies, and all of creation. Jesus has only one plan and that is the Church. There is no alternative plan. He doesn't have an optional military plan, or a last-chance political plan. The Church—a community of the broken and imperfect—is his great plan for all of creation. Jesus' plan and purpose was built on God's work through Israel in the Old Testament. Jesus was a radical, but he was also a reformer. It is important to remember that he was both. God's vision was laid out centuries earlier in prophecies recorded in the Old Testament:

> For as the soil makes the sprout come up
> and a garden causes seeds to grow,
> so the Sovereign LORD will make righteousness
> and praise spring up before all nations. (Is 61:11)

> Is not this the kind of fasting I have chosen:
> to loose the chains of injustice
> and untie the cords of the yoke,
> to set the oppressed free,
> and break every yoke?

Is it not to share your food with the hungry
    and to provide the poor wanderer with shelter—
when you see the naked, to clothe them,
    and not to turn away from your own flesh and blood? (Is 58:6-7)

He was pierced for our transgressions,
    he was crushed for our iniquities;
the punishment that brought us peace was on him,
    and by his wounds we are healed. (Is 53:5)

These few verses from the prophet Isaiah, written over half a millennium before the time of Jesus, point to the very purpose that Jesus identified for his own life and for the lives of his followers. In fact, in Jesus' inaugural address in Luke 4, he quotes directly from this section of Isaiah, as if to say, Here I am! I am the one God has sent to bring this about.

The Spirit of the Lord is on me,
    because he has anointed me
    to proclaim good news to the poor
He has sent me to proclaim freedom for the prisoners
    and recovery of sight for the blind,
to set the oppressed free,
    to proclaim the year of the Lord's favor. (Lk 4:18-19)

Luke makes it very clear that this inaugural address or opening sermon of Jesus was meant to be an announcement: this is what I am going to do; now just watch. The rest of Luke's biography of Jesus and his introduction to the church (the book of Acts) show how Jesus—and the church—begins this movement that we are invited to be part of today. The purpose or mission of Jesus continues through the Church, in general, and through local churches specifically. Some Scriptures, such as John 20:21, make explicit the continuity with Jesus' purpose and method. The resurrected Jesus spoke to his frightened followers: "'As the Father sent me, I am sending you,' And with that he breathed on them and said, 'Receive the Holy Spirit.'" He was addressing his apostles, but by extension he is addressing all of his followers. The foundation of the church is seen it its sentness. The church is a *community sent* by Jesus into the world, as Jesus was sent into the world. As part of the global Church, every local church is not only a local community (institution), but also a movement (a people sent).

In more explicit language we read the purpose of the Church in Matthew 28:16-20. Before looking at this passage, though, we need to pause a moment. When Jesus was preparing to leave earth, to ascend to be with the Father, he left behind (as far as we know) very specific but also very limited plans. He did not tell his followers how to organize themselves. He did not tell them how to run committees, nor did he say what it means to be ordained or whether to meet in the mornings or evenings for worship. He did not even talk about church membership, or the role of women in leadership or how to take offerings. Many people wish he had done so. He left only the instructions that were absolutely necessary. Other instructions, apparently, were not necessary or critical.

Jesus inaugurated the Church through common worship and mission, not in ritual or nuanced beliefs. The Church is constituted in its *adoration of Jesus* (worship) and *commission by Jesus* (mission). We see both *worship* and *witness* as the repeated purposes of the church in numerous passages and in the early church's life. In Matthew 28, one of the most frequently quoted passages, the Church is established: It is established in worship and mission.

> Then the eleven disciples went to Galilee, to the mountain where Jesus had told them to go. When they saw him, *they worshiped him*; but some doubted. Then Jesus came to them and said, "All authority in heaven and on earth has been given to me. *Therefore go and make disciples* of all nations, baptizing them in the name of the Father and of the Son and of the Holy Spirit, and teaching them to obey everything I have commanded you. And surely I am with you always, to the very end of the age." (Mt 28:16-20, italics added)

It is in the midst of *worship* that Jesus gave instructions for *mission* (go) to this fledgling gathering to be called the Church. The overall purpose is to make disciples. The details include baptizing and teaching. The context is that Jesus has all authority and he will be with them to the end. Thus, they are to go to the ends of the earth, and he will accompany them to the end of time. The Church universal begins with a particular church, the left-behind disciples who are told, as they worship, to make disciples of all nations. "All nations" means every language or culture group, not every political nation as we think about nation today. The meaning of this small community is given in their task of reaching out to every single tribe, refugee group, language group, nation on the earth. When you think of it, it was a ridiculous command.

Another passage describes a final scene with Jesus and his disciples. The first chapter of the Acts of the Apostles recounts the episode when Jesus commanded his disciples to wait for the coming of the Holy Spirit before they scatter. Then when they asked if he was going to "restore the kingdom to Israel" (Acts 1:6), continuity with God's work through Israel, he redirected their attention to something far more expansive: "But you will receive power when the Holy Spirit comes on you, and you will be my witnesses in Jerusalem, and in all Judea and Samaria, and to the ends of the earth" (Acts 1:8). Again, Jesus gave extensive and extending directions: To the ends of the earth you will go as witnesses.

A chapter later, in Acts 2, the fulfillment of this begins when the Holy Spirit arrives and people speak in many different languages, almost as a foretelling or a foretaste of their purpose in Jesus' mission. Jesus promised the Holy Spirit, and when the Holy Spirit comes, he comes to aid in *worship* and in *witness*[3] (mission) across cultures. This first community witness occurred during worship. Speaking all the different languages of the Roman Empire and beyond, they were "declaring the wonders of God" (Acts 2:11). Worship and witness, the two primary purposes of the church, also appear in Acts as the two primary themes of the earliest church commissioned by Jesus and experienced by the disciples.

If the *two primary purposes of the church are worship and witness,* how did we end up with such complex churches, denominations, networks, and buildings, not to mention theological statements and theological divisions? Well, it is a long story, and some of this we will talk about in the third chapter, but before that history, I want to take up another important question.

WHY A BASIC BOOK ON THE CHURCH?

Nancy and I learned a great deal visiting thirty-five churches in our first year in California. We learned about both the diversity of expressions of Christian worship and the extent of confusion about "doing church" today. Many diverse movements appear to aim at different purposes and nurture very different goals. What was going on? This seemed so very different from the situation when I was attending church as a child, a period of time when diverse churches shared much more similarity, but that similarity came more from the context of Christendom rather than a shared understanding of the Church. And frankly, even though I saw much more consistency among churches in the twentieth century, the purpose of those churches was not clear to me at the time.

This basic book is for people who, like most people in the West today, are confused or uninformed about the meaning and purpose of church. This is a guide for people who don't naturally, or have not traditionally, "done church." I write it as a person who was also very confused about church when I was young, but I realize that my confusion in the twentieth century is nothing compared with the confusion we have now in the twenty-first century. I hope that high school students who are thinking of joining a church, college students who are studying about Christianity (whether Christian or not), and people who were not raised in a Christian home but who have now come to faith and are joining a church—that all these people will find this guide helpful. For a number of decades now I have thought about church, both globally (in many cultures) and historically (2,000 years).

HOW THIS BOOK IS ORGANIZED

This volume seeks to explain what a local church is to be and what the Church is by using five body movements of worship:

- Come   • Stand   • Kneel   • Sit   • Go

On one level it is very simple. Many Christians take these postures every week in worship, either figuratively or actually. Yes, some churches do actually stand to praise and then sit and kneel. Most newer churches do not, but it was the pattern picked up from Old Testament patterns of worship.[4] We come to worship, we stand to praise God, we kneel to confess our sins, we sit to receive the Word and the elements, and then we go to bring Christ's love to the world. This is pretty straightforward, but it is deceptively simple.

On another level this is very complex, even mysterious. The simple act of coming, chapter two, is more than just coming to worship, it also symbolizes a choice and a calling. We are choosing not to do other things. When we come we are turning to Christ and to the cross, trusting in a different authority and a historic event. Thus, *come* symbolizes conversion to Christ and, thus, to his body, the Church. Each chapter is organized in the same way: we look at a basic body movement in worship and unpack what lies behind that movement and how it reminds us of the nature of the Church, not just the purpose of worship.

This book will irritate most people a little and (hopefully) encourage them a lot. I describe the Church as I have studied it throughout history and throughout the world.[5] I am very fortunate to have had the opportunity (or obligation) to study the Church (and churches) in such a broad context, and I have been blessed to meet many global church leaders as well. Spending much of my working life with "professional Christians" in a seminary, I have asked some family members and friends from around the world to read chapters and make comments. I listed their names in the acknowledgments at the front of this book. Thus, a small community of global Christians has helped to shape the final product. Because of the nature of the Church and because of human nature, none will be fully satisfied. And yet I hope that most, if not all, will see something of their church, and something of what they wish and pray for the global church in the following pages.

Before we look at the five basic body movements of worship, let's begin with a brief sketch of how we got here: from Christian movement to Christendom to post-Christendom.

2

HOW DID WE GET HERE?

From the Jesus Movement, to Christendom, to Post-Christendom

I HAVE COACHED ABOUT THIRTY-FIVE TEAMS in my life: all teams my children were playing on. I was glad to have the time with them, and we had lots of fun and learned a lot about life—mostly, it seems, through the agony of defeat. Most of our teams were like the Chicago Cubs before 2016. That means that we were underachievers, but we were loyal to one another and made great memories. Most churches are also underachievers.

Here is my analogy about church and sports teams, starting with the world's sport: soccer. Before understanding how to improve a soccer team, you need a pretty good analysis of what is wrong. For example, the striker is making bad passes, the sweeper is too slow, the goalie is not communicating with his defense, the midfielder is not passing the ball—these are common problems. So we analyze the problem before making adjustments.

Churches also have problems, and our most basic problem today is simply that of understanding what the Church is. But before we can understand the Church, or before we begin to "fix" our local church as we see fit, we first need to understand a little bit about how we got to this situation. This will not be too painful; it will be a light dose of history in a small chapter. However, I have found this very helpful in understanding how we got from the New Testament to the diverse expressions of church that we have today.

This chapter is based on this one assumption about the Church, an assumption that will guide our discussion for the rest of this book: the Church, and thus each local church, is always *connected* and *contextual*.

Any local church must be *connected* to Jesus and to the earliest church, and it must be *contextually* relevant and meaningful for its location and people. Being connected means that, since the Church is called *the* body of Christ, it must show its unity with Jesus and, at some level, with all Christians. All churches are connected because there is only one Church. Many people have written about what that unity is that keeps us connected,[1] and while this discussion is very much worth having in your local church, it is not one for us now and here. However, if Christianity has no coherence from church to church and throughout time, then we really are not all one body. We actually become different religions with different centers. Thus, any new church being planted, as well as any traditional church contemplating some drastic changes in form, structure, or beliefs, should make sure they stay connected to the family (the body of Christ). The main clue to our connectedness is Jesus Christ. The connection among all churches comes through the life, teachings, death, resurrection, and ascension of Jesus Christ.

But churches are not all exactly the same, and that is one of the reasons for this book. Churches have some major differences. Just think about something as simple and straightforward as collecting the offering. I have worshiped in a church in South Africa where offering was a fifteen-minute event where music guided the parishioners, row by row, to bring up their offerings to two women with large pots in the front of the church. The movement toward the pots was part dance and part march, but all celebration. I have been in a church where someone sang a song that was difficult to understand while men in tuxedos (no lie!) passed brass collection plates with red velvet lining on the inside. Other churches have collection pillars on the way out of the church, and some collect the offering by pushing a plate on a long pole in front of your face. Some churches give very specific instructions about who is to give, and others say nothing. All of these differences are a matter of context. South Africans celebrate offering and do so in a manner consistent with all worship: song and dance. The tuxedo ushers were from a very wealthy section of a major city; the clients (parishioners) expected this type of formality around money. Context determines how we express our worship of Jesus and our witness in each place. And this is just some diversity in collecting the offering. The differences about the Lord's Supper, Communion, or Eucharist are even more complex and divisive.

Thus, as we look at history here, we will see some important themes that keep us connected and should be retained or (if we have lost them) recovered. Other items started out as a matter of context and can be dropped (or maybe even should be dropped). By the end of the chapter we should have a better idea of how we got to where we are in the twenty-first century with our great diversity of churches. By the end of the book we should have an idea of what holds us all together as the Church.

FROM JESUS TO CHURCHES AND THE CHURCH

The Church was Jesus' idea. He gathered some people around him, taught them what to do, sent them out, debriefed, and then he was killed. He explained that what he was beginning was a whole new way of thinking about the world, societies, relationships, and good and evil. He explained that it was the kingdom of God, and his followers were given the task of spreading it. It was not an earthly kingdom, but a powerful kingdom of resistance and joy that permeated all earthly kingdoms. As I said, he was killed, or more accurately, he was nailed to a cross for these ideas, but then he came back to life (surprising absolutely everyone) and gave his followers marching orders: a whole new purpose for life. A mysterious kingdom for this world, and he was the king.

The earliest church spread throughout three continents by people who were so identified with Jesus that they saw their lives as a continuation of the life of Jesus on earth. Driven by the final words of Jesus to his disciples, they did "go" and "make disciples" of many cultures (Mt 28:19). It was costly, unorganized, extensive, and a labor of love. The words of Jesus were translated into Greek, Armenian, Syriac, and soon they were in Arabic, Gothic (German), Ge'ez (Ethiopian), and some of Jesus' teachings were in Chinese. Worship centered on Jesus' words and his life. Central to worship was the Eucharist because it was both commanded by Jesus ("do this in remembrance of me," Lk 22:19), and it reminded the believers every week that Jesus' life culminated in his death for us. Breaking bread and pouring wine reinforced Jesus' meaning. In great contrast to other religions, the followers of Jesus had the dubious joy of remembering their God as one who was crushed and killed. Remembering the cross and passion (suffering) of Jesus every week united the community and reminded all of Jesus' followers of the virtues of humility and faith. It also reminded them that the basic twin problems of humanity, sin and death, were conquered. Death conquered death.

New believers were initiated or received their new identity through baptism.[2] The old was put under the waters (as if killed), and the new person rose up from the cleansing waters (as if a new life). Baptism and Eucharist were two signs (more accurately called *sacraments*[3]) that centered the church on complete identity with Jesus the God-man.

Communities were soon formed in Persia (Syria, Iraq, and Iran) as well as North Africa (Egypt, Nubia, and Ethiopia) and Europe (from the Mediterranean to Britain). Not individuals, but families, villages, and even empires were converted, that is, changed their allegiance to follow Jesus as Lord. Conversion was communal. When new believers turned to reorient their lives around the life of Jesus, the local communities or churches began to develop patterns that could be passed on: patterns for living, for worshiping, and for witnessing. Of course, local contexts and different languages mixed things up a bit[4] and so tensions developed about the proper way to worship, the proper way to express beliefs, and how to live as a Christian.

> More than anything else, it was worship that normed Christian theology.

Worship language (much of it from the New Testament) indicated the identity of Jesus ("[He is] in very nature God. . . . Every tongue [will] acknowledge that Jesus Christ is Lord," Phil 2:6, 11). The language of Jesus as Lord was dominant in worship. For the early Jewish Christians, *Lord* (*kyrios* in Greek) was the word that was used for God (YHWH) in the Septuagint (Greek Old Testament). *Lord* meant God. Jesus, the human who spoke Aramaic and ate local olives, drank wine, and had a mother named Mary, was God in human form. The diverse church spreading across three continents was united in worship even as they struggled to explain the full meaning of what was foundational. The common assumption that this message should be translated into each language added another layer of complexity to this mission. Common liturgies (patterns in worship) kept beliefs common, connected, and centered on Jesus.

Looking back: The Church's connection to Israel. As we have seen, Jesus, a Jew, came to speak first to the Jewish leaders, and then his movement was intentionally sent out to all cultures (nations). However, the Jewish background laid the foundation for the Church. The understanding of God as creator, as One God, the basic Law and commandments (found in Deuteronomy) were all still important in Jesus' teachings. From the Old Testament sacrifice the early church understood the meaning of Jesus' death. "Look, the Lamb of God, who takes away the sin of the world!" (Jn 1:29). This exclamation from John the Baptist referred to the concept of sacrifice given to Israel as a way to remove sins. The Law commanded that animals be sacrificed, but at the critical point of Israel's liberation or redemption from Egypt, a lamb was sacrificed at Passover. The death and blood of the innocent lamb marked the family for life and freedom (Ex 12).

The early Jewish Christians understood this well, and so throughout its history, the Church has continued to identify Jesus as the Lamb of God. Even in Revelation, looking ahead into the heavenly realm, John "sees" Jesus as the Lamb: "Then I saw a Lamb, looking as if it had been slain, standing at the center of the throne, encircled by the four living creatures and the elders" (Rev 5:6). The victorious God (Lord) is identified in his humiliation and apparent defeat. And so, throughout history Christian worship has retained this Jewish element.

Many other elements of the Old Testament are also foundational for the Christian Church. The idea of testament or covenant comes from God's covenant with Israel. We read of a "new covenant" in Jeremiah 31:31, and the early church identified Jesus as that new covenant. Thus, as early as the third century, the biographies (Gospels) and significant letters about Jesus began to be called the New Testament. Jesus is also identified as the Good Shepherd, and early Christians were quick to see that Psalm 23 was speaking of Jesus. First Peter identifies Jesus as the cornerstone—the foundation—for some and a "stone that causes people to stumble" (1 Pet 2:7-8) for others. This language also comes from Jewish Scriptures: "but for both Israel and Judah he will be a stone that causes people to stumble and a rock that makes them fall" (Is 8:14).

The very language of worship, the benedictions (good words) in worship also use blessings directly from Old Testament writings:

> The LORD bless you
>   and keep you;
> the LORD make his face shine on you
>   and be gracious to you;
> the LORD turn his face toward you
>   and give you peace. (Num 6:24-26)

In short, the Christian church in worship develops and completes the idea of worship (sacrifice, song, poetry, liturgy) found in the Hebrew Scriptures. The Old Testament is a foretaste of worship fulfilled in Jesus Christ. Theology, right thinking about God, was first expressed in worship.

Looking forward: Theology and worship as one. Thus, theology was developed from worship, and worship was the community expression of thanksgiving for what God had done. Christian worship was a radical new expression of Israel's worship, now with a sense of *completion* and *mission*. The response to God's grace led to an expression of belief. Worship was always fully, completely, thoroughly, directly, and indirectly about Jesus. He was the promised Messiah, which means "anointed one." In Greek, the word is *christos*. Followers were called Christians because they were identified with Jesus Christ. Worship traced his life, teachings, suffering, death, resurrection, and ascension. In the single worship event on the day of resurrection (Sunday), as well as throughout the Christian year, Jesus' life and teachings made up the content of worship. Thus, worship affirmed the full divinity of Jesus, his human suffering, his death for our sins, and his conquest over death. When questions were raised—How could he really be a human if he was raised from the dead?—worship language re-centered the discussions.

Disagreements about Jesus' identity continued for hundreds of years, for his identity as fully human and fully divine both confounded scholars and inspired worship. Another major struggle arose concerning God: If Jesus was really God, then who is God? Is God a mode of existence who can be a Spirit and then (like a Transformer) turn into a human Jesus and then into the Creator? Are there three Gods? Language of God as three persons who is still one God began to develop, but this formulation became necessary because of worship language. The worshiping church called upon the Holy Spirit as if actually calling upon God. They directed prayer to Jesus or prayed in Jesus' name. So who is God? The answer given and affirmed in worship was clear: God is a triune person, a three-in-one God. And so the earliest statements of belief, centered on the historic Jesus, guided the church, and the church recited them in worship. The Apostles' Creed[5] is one of the most important and most quoted.

> I believe in God the Father Almighty, Creator of heaven and earth.
>
> I believe in Jesus Christ, His only Son, our Lord.
> He was conceived by the power of the Holy Spirit, and born of the Virgin Mary.
> He suffered under Pontius Pilate, was crucified, died and was buried.
> He descended to the dead.[6]
> On the third day he rose again.
> He ascended into heaven and is seated at the right hand of the Father.
> He will come again to judge the living and the dead.[7]
>
> I believe in the Holy Spirit, the holy catholic[8] church,
> The communion of saints, the forgiveness of sins,
> The resurrection of the body, and the life everlasting.

Three paragraphs about the three-person God. The center of belief (what we confess to be true; our confession), like the center of worship, is Jesus.

If we have been following this carefully it may appear that our discussion has veered away from our original statement that the Church has two and only two abiding purposes: worship and witness. Here we are only talking about belief. I think it is best to think of the struggle to norm Christian beliefs as a missionary encounter with cultures and philosophies. It is very likely that this *creed* ("I believe") was first a public declaration given at baptism. Today public confession of belief, especially on secular university campuses, is a type of witness. Confession points to Jesus, and witness means giving out witness of what Jesus has done and who Jesus is. Every time the gospel encounters a new language, a new culture, is a missionary encounter. Every conversion and confession is a witness to Jesus Christ.

This discussion is important for a basic guide to the church because we must remember that it is possible to get belief wrong and then to worship a false Jesus, or to worship a generic God. Worship should always be, as in the early church, a time of re-centering our belief and our witness.

One quick example will help. The creed above gives minimal information about Jesus. There were people who could affirm most of what this statement says but who developed a belief, contrary to the teaching of Scripture, that Jesus was himself a creation. Jesus came into existence inside of Mary, and this was when he was "created." Many people reasoned, as Arius[9] and others in the fourth century, that Jesus was created, born, lived, and then was exalted to live in close fellowship with God because of his holy life. It was reasonable, but it was not what Jesus or the apostles Paul, Peter, or John had taught. It was also not what the worship and liturgy taught.[10] After much discussion, councils, and not a few angry words, statements like the following were developed to reflect what Scripture taught and what worship celebrated:

I believe in one God the Father Almighty; Maker of heaven and earth, and of all things visible and invisible.

And in one Lord Jesus Christ, the only-begotten Son of God, begotten of the Father before all worlds, God of God, Light of Light, very God of very God, begotten not made, being of one substance [essence] with the Father; by whom all things were made.[11]

This statement from the Council of Nicaea held in 325, overseen by Emperor Constantine, ruled out any question about Jesus' origin: Being fully God, he could not be created, but he was "begotten" from before all words. Jesus is "very God of very God." Worship practices in the Eucharist, baptism, and other elements of the liturgy had all taught this about Jesus. Now it was sealed in a confession. False teachings, such as those of Arius, called for responses, and the responses were given as orthodox (*ortho-doxa*: right or straight opinion or worship). Worship, the gathering of the local Christian community, would re-center Christian belief each week around the grace of God in Jesus and the practices expected to flow from this belief.

> Right teaching became right praise or glory. Worship expressed orthodox theology and repressed false teaching.

Looking outward: From persecution to protection. While the growing church was establishing common beliefs and practices in worship, it was also struggling for survival. At first persecution came from the Jews (Christian belief seemed to be a heresy of Jewish beliefs), but soon persecution came from imperial regimes: the Roman Empire and the Persian Empire. Both Jesus and Paul had promised persecution and suffering for the followers of Jesus (Mt 10:22; 16:24-26; Phil 1:29; 2 Tim 3:12). That is exactly what happened. In many regions Christians had to worship secretly in homes, and during certain periods and various places, authorities rounded up Christians and killed them. Political rulers were to be feared. Yet even with the threats of persecution, the young Christian movement grew. Christians talked about the dead savior who was alive. Their changed lives made up part of the message. We even read in places how the love that Christians showed the poor, the orphans, and widows angered government officials: "They even take care of our poor!" complained one official.[12] Thus, in the first few centuries, being a Christian went against the cultural norms. In many cases it was dangerous to confess Jesus as Lord. Still the good news (gospel) of Jesus spread, and more and more local churches were founded. Jesus and the love of the Jesus communities proved to be winsome to the ancient world.

Then something unexpected happened. Before Christianity was even a large minority of the population of the Roman Empire—in the early fourth century—the emperor (Constantine) became a Christian, and he began to remove all restrictions against the church. In fact the empire became a friend of the church. The empire would provide buildings and vessels for worship. Sunday was declared a holiday for worship. Churches and priests did not have to pay taxes. Less than three centuries after the death and resurrection of Jesus, Christians were protected. Not only did Christianity soon become the protected religion, Christians were favored in the palace, and other religions began to be persecuted. In fact, some Christians became comfortable and wealthy, and some of their leaders began to wield political power. This was not the life that Jesus had foretold for his followers: "Blessed are you when people insult you, persecute you and falsely say all kinds of evil against you because of me" (Mt 5:11).

Some Christians, seeking to live a life fully devoted to Jesus in an age of affluence and ease, fled to the desert to live a more austere "Christlike" life. Monasteries spread rapidly, not only in the Roman Empire, but even beyond. It is not really that hard to understand this today. The world and its affluence was infecting the church, making it difficult to be fully devoted to Jesus and his mission. The early church, as we read in Acts, often sold their goods to care for each other and to feed to poor. Now the government was subsidizing the church. Following Jesus became more than acceptable; it became popular.

This situation in the West, where the government and church mutually support one another, has become known as Christendom. In Christendom, the church has power, influence, and the ability to use that power in unchristian ways. It often did. Christendom is an alliance between church and state. The state assumes the Christian belief and practice of its citizens—as normal—and the church accepts (even expects!) the support of the state. In short, Christianity holds a special status, and other beliefs face restrictions and, many times, persecution.

Christendom made it possible for the church to survive, and it was a great opportunity for the church to grow. Centuries of persecution had ended. We must not be overly critical of Christendom because basic values of respect for God, the church, the family, sabbath rest, and other Christian virtues had support within Christendom. However, Christendom also misrepresented Jesus, the humble savior of the world.

Worldly power and pride were constant temptations, even infections of the church. This odd arrangement of Jesus and worldly power constituted the history of Christianity in the West from the fourth

> It is important to remember that Christendom always bends the church toward persecution of others and hubris of its own.

through most of the twentieth century. That favorable status that the church had for so many centuries is now gone. We now live in a post-Christendom age. Our situation in relationship to governments and cultures bears greater resemblance to that of the very early church than to the church of the Reformation or even the early twentieth century. Many Christians in the West have not yet understood the dramatic change that has taken place.

CHURCH AS SIGNPOST OF THE KINGDOM

Now that local churches no longer serve as representatives of cultures or governments, they function as outposts or signposts to the world. As outposts they are present in foreign territory, bringing good news and relief to those in need. As signposts, they point the way to God and his loving and gracious kingdom. Christian communities stand out as something new and different, as something hopeful. The local church should now be a hopeful sign in an age of violence, division, and affluence.

One helpful way to look at this is to remember that for most of humanity a nation or people had their own culture: language, food, myths, and worship united a people. A nation was united in the worship of their god or goddess (often a number of each) who gave them their identity. You become what you worship (more on this to come). Thus, cultures differed by cultural practices related to worship: Athena for the Athenians, Lug for the Celts, Thor for the Germanic people, Marduk (among others) for the Babylonians.[13] Christians proclaimed in their worship and practice that Jesus was the savior God for all people: Greeks, Celts, Germans, Franks, and even Babylonians or Persians. The life of the Christians contrasted with the life of surrounding people, whether they were in Egypt, Libya, Persia, Asia Minor, or Ireland. A number of writings of the first centuries expressed their countercultural way of life and worship, both as a defense of their belief and an explanation of their practices. These writings explained that *Christians were not an ethnic group* but were found in all cultures, and they contributed to those cultures.

> For Christians cannot be distinguished from the rest of the human race by country or language or customs. They do not live in cities of their own; they do not use a peculiar form of speech; they do not follow an eccentric manner of life. . . . Although they live in Greek and barbarian cities alike, as each man's lot has been cast, and follow the customs of the country in clothing and food and other matters of daily living, at the same time they give proof of the remarkable and admittedly extraordinary constitution of their own commonwealth. They live in their own countries, but only as aliens. . . . Every foreign land is their fatherland, and yet for them fatherland is a foreign land. They marry, like everyone else, and they beget children, but they do not cast out their offspring. They share their board with each other, but not their marriage bed.[14]

In other words, Christian communities lived in and among the common population, dressing the same way and eating most of the same food, but their morals were different (higher). They did not kill unwanted children and they were chaste in marriage. As we read later in this early Christian document, "They obey the established laws, but in their own lives they go far beyond what the laws require."[15]

Such an understanding of the church in the world was expressed in recent decades by J. E. Lesslie Newbigin,[16] who said that the church is to be present in the world as a "signpost" of the kingdom of God. Actually Newbigin went a bit further and said the local church is a signpost, a foretaste, and an instrument of the kingdom of God.[17] Thus, each local church does not serve itself, but points beyond itself and is much bigger than itself. In confession of its belief, the local church is pointing to a greater reality where God reigns as Father, Son, and Holy Spirit over all of creation. In celebrating the Eucharist (Communion) the church points to a future where there will be no more death or suffering. In providing a community where all are welcome through the grace and mercy of a God who died for us, the church is a foretaste of God's kingdom of love. When the local church helps in healing family feuds, and when church members hold the abused and wounded, and when the homeless find a "home" with a local congregation, then the church is an instrument of the kingdom of God. Such a community is Jesus (the body of Christ) for any local town, village, or city. A person from a city might ask where is God in such a violent and careless world, and people should be able to point to a local church and say, "I am not sure, but I think that church is the best clue we have." In a pre-Christendom world as well as a post-Christendom world, this description of the church in the world holds tremendous illumination.

THE JOY AND PAIN OF CHRISTENDOM

But how did we get from local churches that were models of something different—something more loving and gracious than the local society—to a religion that wielded worldly power? Christianity was not the majority faith of the Roman Empire when Emperor Constantine decided to support Christianity. Christians were still a very marginalized minority who were often persecuted for their beliefs into the fourth century. Constantine's conversion has been criticized much in recent decades, and yet with his change of heart everything changed about Christianity in the West. Everything changed.

Upon Emperor Constantine's conversion, Christianity spread across the empire, and each local church stepped into a new historic trajectory.[18] Suddenly Christian leaders who had been tortured were invited to discuss theology at the emperor's palace in Nicaea. Men who had been blinded or had their ears cut off for confessing Christ were suddenly heroes and leaders. Sunday became a sacred day; many churches received imperial funding for their buildings; and Christianity became identified with the empire rather than with a rejected itinerant Jewish prophet.

It is easy to see how important this change was for Western Christianity because in Asia (Persia), where Christianity was never supported by the empire, Christianity constantly struggled for survival and—to this day—has never flourished. Christendom helped Christianity survive, but, we might ask, how did that political and economic support change Christianity? Christianity became a royal religion where popes would crown kings, and kings began to choose bishops. The image of Pope Leo III crowning Charlemagne as king of the Franks on Christmas Day, 799, is a famous image that communicates how Christendom rulers were understood to be responsible to God through God's vicar, the pope.

As late as the 1950s and 1960s this relationship between church, state, and citizens was still assumed in Europe. The recent television production about the life of Queen Elizabeth (who became queen at the age of twenty-six!) expresses this well as the queen's grandmother tells her about her ultimate responsibility to God, for the sake of the nation and the people. This, or something similar, was spoken to the young queen around 1951:

QUEEN ELIZABETH: In your letter that you sent to me, you said, "Loyalty, to the ideal you have inherited, is your duty above everything else, because the calling comes from the highest source; from God himself."

QUEEN MARY: Yes.

ELIZABETH: Do you really believe that?

MARY: Monarchy is God's sacred mission to grace and dignify the earth; to give ordinary people an ideal to strive towards . . . an example of nobility and duty to raise them in their wretched lives. Monarchy is a calling from God: that is why you are crowned in an abbey, not in a government building; why you are anointed and not appointed. It's an archbishop who puts your crown on your head,

not a minister or a public servant, which
means that you are answerable to God in your
duty, not the public.

ELIZABETH: I am not sure my husband would agree
                              with that![19]

Churches existing in Christendom had a certain dignity, responsibility,
and shared authority in culture and the larger society—at least *at their
best* they did. For those of us in the West, this is now our history. When
I was growing up (in the twentieth century) it was my reality.

CHURCHES IN DECLINE; CHRISTIANITY REBORN

It is important to know some of this history to understand why this book
was written; many of the assumptions about the church that were true in
the twentieth century no longer hold true today. We need to understand
why we see such diverse images and practices of churches today, in a day
after the end of Christendom, and the Western church seeks a new place
and identity. Many, if not most, churches in the West today still function
on the Christendom model and understanding. In Christendom, the
broader culture supported Christian values and virtues. Thus, much of
the work of the church was done by local schools, courts, and even television! That's right. Up until the late twentieth century, television programs upheld the values of truth-telling, marriage, family accountability,
respect for the elderly, and even praying at mealtime and attending
church. Shows depicted priests and pastors as positive models of
Christian life.

To be frank, there was much confusion. Many of the values of the
larger society were not Christian even though the society was a
Christendom culture. And many of the habits and prejudices of the
church were less than Christian too. The broader culture spewed forth
both clean and brackish water. Often the church hardly did much better.
Popular Western culture tended to be racist and to devalue the role of
women in society. Churches formed part of the mainstream, so what was
Christian and what was Western culture melded together.

As churches decline and close in the West (and at the same time different types of churches are being planted and growing) it is a good time to ask, What is the Church? The follow-up question relates more directly to this volume: What does a church look like and what does it do?

WE'VE GOT A LOT IN COMMON:
CHURCH IN THE SECOND AND TWENTY-FIRST CENTURIES

I do believe that rather than thinking about revising or reforming the Christendom churches that exist it is more helpful to rethink church as it was from the beginning, from the early church, since that situation has more in common with our present context. In our present context, like that of the early church, the church is an outsider in a very pluralistic world dominated by clashing empires. The church was essentially a missionary institution in a religiously pluralistic world. In the second or third century, a young Christian attending a local Christian assembly would be participating in a countercultural—even illegal—activity. Nothing, or at least very little, in the larger society would support the teachings and activity of a local church. This would have been true in Persia (present-day Iran and Syria), in North Africa, in Turkey, or in southern France. For periods of time and in certain places (geographically), Christian worship would be tolerated, but you could never be sure if that would still be the case next year or even next week or in the next town. That seems so far from our situation in the West today, and yet, it is not so different. As we noted above, the local church (as well as the Church in the world) must see itself more as an outpost and signpost of the kingdom than as an expression of and support for the larger culture. The church has little favored status in society.

All this means that, as Christians, we lead a life closer to that of the early church than of the twentieth, nineteenth, or even the sixteenth century. Today, a Christian is declaring loyalty to another authority and kingdom, and this may be very threatening to our earthly rulers and their laws and mores. In almost every country in the world today, Christianity is at most tolerated and more likely restrained or persecuted. Like the early church, local churches today confess among each other their beliefs and confess to the world a message that may be a threat to local norms and rulers. The church in North America or Europe will increasingly have more of a marginal existence, more like the church in India, Vietnam, or China than like the Western church of the past.

NOW WE CAN LOOK AT THE CHURCH

With this brief historical background we now have some tools to use in thinking about church today. For example, we have seen that the earliest communities understood the church as the local gathering to engage in witness. The first word in these churches was *go*. They understood that they were continuing the work of Jesus in the world. The church is a witness to Jesus. And so we can ask, Is this still part of the DNA of our church today? Should it be? What would this look like in the twenty-first century?

We have also seen how churches have argued and divided and even fought (I mean real wars!) over theological and cultural issues. Few of these battles were purely spiritual or theological, and all of these battles hurt the witness of the church. Witness is one of the two major purposes of the church. And so as we look at the following chapters and think about our own churches, we might ask, Are we divisive and pugnacious as a local church? Do we create greater unity, or do we constantly promote our own uniqueness, encouraging greater division?

Also from the past, we see how the church has worked very closely with the broader culture and with political leaders. Christendom cultures assumed that rulers were Christians and Christian life was national life. Jesus was seen more as a king than as a humble shepherd. This is not our world today. So how does the church relate to the larger culture and to political rulers? Is the church an isolated island of Christian life, or can and should the local church relate to political leaders, and even look for the conversion of local cultures? Or, to return to the first page of this chapter, how is the Church and our local church both *connected* to Jesus and that earliest tradition and at the same time relevant to the local *context*?

Keeping these themes and lessons from church history in our minds, we now turn to look at the five basic movements of the church. The first movement represents conversion as well as the simple choice to go to church on a Sunday morning (or evening) rather than going to play golf, shopping, or going to the coffee shop to sip coffee and read the Sunday *Times*. *Come* means come to Jesus and come to his body, the church.

3

COME

IT WAS A TERRIBLE STORY OF EVANGELISM—the type of evangelism that ends up as a parody in bad movies about corrupt evangelists and greedy preachers. A twenty-something man strode through the university campus one afternoon at a fairly rapid pace. Looking intent and prophet-like, he sternly shouted out to people, "Repent! Repent from your sins." He didn't stop to engage people, he just shouted his call to repentance and went on before anyone could ask questions or offer a challenge. He was known as the "crazy prophet." Angry, detached, accusing, he was anything but a bearer of good news.

Well, actually, the crazy prophet *did* engage one person, and it changed his life. A young man who was in a terrible place in life came out of a class building and looked the prophet straight in his eyes. The prophet looked at him and with no hesitation said, "Do you know Jesus as your Lord and Savior?" The dejected student had no time to improvise. He just uncharacteristically spoke honestly, "No, I don't." The prophet replied, "Well you better get to know him," and then he was off to his next uncomfortable audience. The student, we will call him Mark, went back to his fraternity house—half home, half destruction zone—went up to his room, found a Bible and started reading Jesus' words from the Gospels. As Mark told me three years later when he was a seminary student,

> That afternoon, alone in my bunk, I read the most beautiful words I had ever
> seen. My life was one of deception. Jesus spoke the truth. My life was one of
> pride, posturing, and threats. Jesus was humble, honest and vulnerable. I
> knew immediately that who Jesus was, I wanted to be, and what he thought,

I wanted to think. I didn't know what it meant, but right then and there—with all the smell of stale beer and in the midst of broken furniture, I prayed something that basically said, "I give up, Jesus. Help me." And so I did—and he did.

It didn't matter that I had a messed up life at that time. I had court appearances for my violent lifestyle as a bouncer for our fraternity. I knew I was failing out of college, again. And then my family relationships were so unhealthy; I guess we call it dysfunctional today. All of that faded in the background because now all I saw was the beauty and purity of Jesus. It was that vision, maybe not so much of a vision, but that person I had been reading about who was pulling me forward. All other problems and relationships were overwhelmed by this one new relationship. With all of my personal issues still pressing in on me, I was at peace for the first time I could remember.

Come means more than one thing:

- We come to Jesus: conversion.
- We come to the body of Christ: community.
- We come to worship: identity.

This chapter looks at all these dimensions of what it means to come. But come does mean conversion, the beautiful start of a new life, with new family and with a new purpose for life. It's true: conversion is beautiful.

WHAT IS CONVERSION?

The story above is a composite of two or three stories that I heard from converts in the past twenty years of listening to conversion stories. It is remarkable that such a confrontational approach was so used by God to bring a hardened heart to a tender faith in Jesus. For the record, we do not recommend such a confrontational approach in evangelism, but we do recommend living an evangelistic lifestyle. Although many books have been written on conversion and much study done about how and why people come to faith in Jesus, it is still a mystery and a miracle how and when a person or family comes to faith. However, at some point a person has to come to the place where she or he will say to God (and then to others), I have decided to trust my life to Jesus and no longer live on my own, alone. It is a statement of surrender and a new identity. It is both: a death and new life.

In coming to Jesus we surrender the independence we have assumed and that society expects of us. In most Western societies, whether typified by Latino *machismo* or the rugged American individualist (think Hollywood or professional sports heroes), we value independence and strength of character. But conversion works from completely different assumptions. To trust Jesus we must admit our need, our sin, and we must surrender our independence. We must even surrender our cultural images of what it means to be fully *me*. We are saying simply, "I can't, but he can."

When we come to church we are not just coming to worship; we are coming, or joining, a new community. Yes, coming to Jesus is joining (for the rest of eternity) a cosmic body that we see and experience locally and finitely. We each find out that this community is made of people just like me. Everyone in this community is insecure and needy; everyone has given up. We are a community of the sur-rendered. It may sound a little

> Conversion is surrender. It is surrender to the one who can save us, who can comfort and guide us. But it is also surrender into our true identity, which is not found in us alone, but in God. We become our true selves, and our true selves are more glorious than we ever could have imagined before.

depressing to be with so many defeated people, but it is actually a sweet aroma to the world. A group of people who no longer have to pretend to be what they are not: independent, self-sufficient, and self-authenticating. What a burden to have to pretend that "I am my own." What a relief and joy to be with honest, humble, broken people who can say, like Mark, "I can't, but he can."

I gave a talk in Beijing to a Sunday school class that was made up mostly of Chinese who had studied overseas or who were from overseas (Malaysia, Singapore, Taiwan, etc.). Some local Chinese students also attended. After the class a young professional woman came up and asked a fairly basic question about following Jesus. Knowing that there were many people who come to these classes searching for faith, I asked her if she was a Christian. "I don't know, I don't think I am there yet," she replied. After hearing her questions, I felt she would soon be definite about that. But at this point, she knew that she had not turned, or surrendered. Some people will come to worship to be in a Christian community, and later they will actually come to Jesus.

Another woman in Asia, a person well-placed in the government who had gone through some recent loss, talked to me for a few hours over two pots of tea. Her remarkable sharing from the heart revealed a person with much worldly power and influence, but on a personal level—like so many of us—she was broken and in need of support. She had nowhere to turn and no one to turn to. I talked about trusting Jesus with her loneliness, pain, and loss. Two days later she came back to me, I prayed for her, she thanked me, and then she quietly said, "I don't think I am there yet." I knew her meaning. She had not experienced conversion yet, but she was close.

Conversion is both a process and an event. For some people, like the present author, conversion can be dated because everything became different all at once. At the age of sixteen, in a friend's living room (not at church), I was told that Jesus' life presents a question to each of us. "Right," I said. "What is the question?" Very simply, I was told it presents the question, "Will you follow me?" As long as we do not answer that question, as long as we sit on the fence or sit in the judgment seat, we have answered No. I had read enough about the Gospels, and I knew myself well enough to know right then and there that I wanted to answer Yes. I needed a savior and I was not embarrassed about it at all. That evening, after thinking about it all day, I wanted to nail it down, so I rolled over in bed, looked up at the top bunk and said something like "Jesus, here I am. Take me." It was inarticulate, it lacked panache and nuance, but it was memorable—unforgettable in fact.

Two things happened. First, I immediately had this clear under-standing that when I was twice my age then (that is, at the ripe old age of thirty-two!) I would still be making decisions based upon this decision.

I knew the course of my life had changed. Second, I opened my Bible and did a very immature thing, but God seemed to understand. I opened my Bible to the Gospels and hoped that I would find a verse to hold on to. God met my silliness with his wisdom. My eyes focused on Luke 9:62, and they still do. "Jesus said to him, 'No one who puts his hand to the plow and looks back is fit for the kingdom of heaven.'" I am now nearly four times as old as when I came to faith in Christ, and this verse still is with me, and I am still making decisions based upon that one decision made in October of 1970. I am getting so old, but God is still so fresh.

I experienced conversion as an event, but even mine and every other conversion involves a process or ongoing turnings in our lives. Years after coming to faith we can look back and see the many times we made turns, or we were being turned to God, by God's invisible hand or small voice speaking to us. This reality is not bound by culture at all. It is the universal experience of all who come to faith. In the New Testament we read about Saul, who was watching Stephen being stoned to death (Acts 7:58-60). Could this have been part of his conversion story? When he was blinded on the road to Damascus, when exactly was he converted (Acts 9)? When he heard a voice asking why he was killing people? When he was blinded? Or was he not converted until he regained his sight and Ananias, the reluctant evangelist, explained to Saul that he had been sent to restore his sight? Or was he not really converted until he spent several days with the disciples in Damascus?

The point is that Saul was becoming Paul with each of these events and each of these relationships. On one level his conversion was miraculous. But on another level, Saul's conversion, like all, was a multilayered process that may have a sudden turning, but always turns to the body of Christ. Conversion is to, or into, the Church. This is why the simple word come is a good reminder of the foundation for the Christian life, which is the foundation of the Church. Conversion may be very personal, yet it is also very communal. Thank God.

Conversion brings us into a family that is required to love us. We need that.

Here is another way to view conversion. Conversion is coming to the foot of the cross and allowing God to lift all of our sins, our guilt, our burdens off our backs, and God takes them all upon himself. A very famous image of this comes from John Bunyan's *Pilgrim's Progress*.[1] The main character in the novel, Pilgrim, comes to the cross, trudging along with a huge sack on his back, which makes it nearly impossible for him to go forward. Struggling, he travels along, encouraged by his advocate and companion on his journey, Evangelist. Slowly he comes up to the cross and as soon as he approaches it, the great burden on his back is loosed, it slips off and rolls into a cave whereupon a stone rolls in front of the cave (tomb) and the burdens are seen no more. This is a helpful and instructive image of our coming to the foot of the cross. When we come to the Church (conversion), as well as come to church (worship), we come to the cross. We don't come as a lone individual, but we come to this great community of the beloved, the great family of the forgiven from every tribe and nation. With sin and guilt removed, we are free to relate as whole and healed individuals. Conversion, like worship, is coming to the cross.

COMING TO JESUS THROUGH THE WATERS: BAPTISM

Coming to church is most concretely expressed in true turning to Jesus Christ in baptism.

Baptism symbolizes that coming to Jesus is not a little thing. The turn to Jesus has cosmic dimensions because it is a change in loyalty, a turning around in direction. It short, it is a life-and-death matter (actually a *death-to-life* matter). Baptism, since the earliest followers of Jesus, has been done by pouring water over an infant, child, or adult. It has also been done by going "down to the river" and being plunged under flowing waters. The waters symbolize cleansing from sin (our basic human problem) and washing away even the guilt that results from sin. Water also symbolizes going down in death (under the waters) and rising up to new life. Some churches have a small font of holy water at the entrance of the sanctuary for the Christian, as she enters, to touch the water and then either apply it to her head or cross herself to remind her every time she enters that she has a new identity. "Remember your baptism."

We often forget that turning *to* always and necessarily involves at the same time turning *from*. Coming to Christ is a turning to Jesus and a turning away from evil. Most baptismal liturgies[2] that go back to the early church (a connection with the whole Church) make this very clear.

MINISTER:	Do you, therefore, renounce the devil and all his works, the vain pomp and glory of the world, with all covetous desires of the same, and the sinful desires of the flesh, so that you will not follow, nor be led by them?
ANSWER:	I renounce them all; and by God's help, will endeavor not to follow, nor to be led by them.
MINISTER:	Do you believe in Jesus Christ, the Son of the living God?
ANSWER:	I do.[3]

This clearly shows that we first turn from and then turn to "Jesus Christ, the Son of the living God." It is especially necessary today when we come to Jesus to identify exactly what we are turning from. Western societies no longer support and nurture the Christian life as they did in the past. So we must acknowledge that we are now turning away from much of our society and local cultural norms when we turn to Christ. We are renouncing the devil who works in tempting us to avarice (love of money), passions (in our oversexed society), and egoism (what the early Christians called "self-esteem"). With the ubiquity of materialistic, violent, and sexual images, we need to make a public statement that we are renouncing all these powers and turning to trust the powerful Lord of the universe who took our sins upon himself.

It would be totally appropriate today, in connection with our past (remember this connection in chapter one?), to be a little more explicit in renouncing "the Devil and his works" in our present context.

MINISTER:	Do you, therefore, renounce the devil and all his works: accumulating wealth, watching and thinking about violent and sexual images, placing nationalism over the Kingdom of God, and making a name for yourself instead of proclaiming the name of Jesus Christ?
ANSWER:	I renounce them all; and by God's help, will endeavor not to follow, nor to be led by them.
MINISTER:	Do you believe in Jesus Christ, the Son of the living God?
ANSWER:	Absolutely!

Baptism is very important in almost every church family in the world. Jesus submitted to it and he commanded that it be the sign of entrance into his kingdom (Mt 28:19). Many discussions, conferences, writings, and even church unions in the twentieth century have involved both how to practice baptism and what it means. Churches administer baptism in different ways, but the purpose and basic meaning is commonly understood. It is the public sign of a new loyalty and a new life!

In most cultures of the world, conversion is not an individual choice, but a family, community, or village decision. Thus, families come to the cross as a corporate body. The matriarch or patriarch and all the children, relatives, and servants are baptized at the same time. In our modern, very individualistic culture, we assume that an individual person can decide on his or her own what to do. Many, if not most, people in the West who come to the cross do so on their own. Still we have the tradition of a family baptizing their young child (infant), which is a communal practice. Then, when the child comes of age (twelve–sixteen), the young person affirms, or confirms, his or her faith publically (individual). In all these cases, practicing baptism *connects* us to Jesus and the early church, but the specific practice is also *contextual*. The following quotation may seem a little archaic to us today, but it expresses almost poetically the meaning of baptism. This is from a fifth-century writer:

Divine grace confers on us two gifts through the baptism of regeneration, one being infinitely superior to the other. *The first gift is given to us at once*, when grace renews us in the actual waters of baptism and cleanses all the lineaments of our soul, that is, the image of God in us, by washing away every stain of sin. The second—our likeness to God—*requires our cooperation*. When the intellect begins to perceive the Holy Spirit with full consciousness, we should realize that grace is beginning to paint the divine likeness over the divine image in us. Artists first draw the outline of a man in monochrome, and then add one color after another, until little by little they capture the likeness of the subject down to the smallest details. In the same way the grace of God starts by remaking the divine image in man into what it was when he was first created.[4]

Baptism has always been a sign of God's grace: we are accepted and cleansed by God. It is also the sign of a new beginning—a new life beginning.

I attended the baptism of about fifteen Chinese, mostly scholars from China who were studying or teaching in Pittsburgh, Pennsylvania. Each person to be baptized came from either very strongly atheistic, Maoist families, or moderately nonreligious families. Each person gave a testimony of what coming to Jesus (and this particular church) had meant to him or her. They described a "whole new life," "new possibilities," "new directions," and a "new family." It was an amazing time of celebration and rejoicing. But it was even bigger than what we saw that Sunday morning. In addition, as Luke tells us, "In the same way, I tell you, there is rejoicing in the presence of the angels of God over one sinner who repents" (Lk 15:10). Conversion, repentance, and baptism is one really big thing.

COMING TO JESUS, AGAIN AND AGAIN

Although baptism is a once-and-for-all event, it symbolizes a lifestyle of repentance and constant returning to the cross as described in the quotation above. Baptism both confirms or seals us as people who are now in Christ, and it points to our identity as people in need of cleansing. Living this Christian life has been described in various ways. Here is how a seventeenth-century Roman Catholic reformer described it:

> Therefore we are united with him in the most intimate union possible, that is,
> the union of the members with their head. We are united with him spiritually
> by faith and by the grace he gave us in holy baptism. We are united with him
> bodily in the union of his most sacred body with ours in the holy Eucharist.
> It follows necessarily from this that, just as bodily members are animated by
> the spirit of their head and live its life, in the same way we must be animated
> by the spirit of Jesus, and live his life and walk in his ways. . . . In a word, we
> should continue and bring to fulfillment the life, religion and devotion with
> which he lived on earth.[5]

Coming to Christ brings about a change in our life as our life is now
"hidden with Christ in God" (Col 3:3), and yet the work is not done. We,
and everyone else in our worship service, are still in need of correction.
Still, the work has begun as together we grow into God's greater purposes.

"Remembering our baptism" is not just a trite saying or a ritual; it is
our vital line to Jesus. We remember that we deserve the death that Jesus
died for us. We remember that we were saved by grace and we live by
grace every day. We remember that we need Jesus, and whenever we feel
we are OK on our own, we are in need of his compassion or mercy and
his power.

Conversion, and subsequent baptism, is both a once-and-for-all event
and also a continual way of living. Symbolically, each Sunday morning,
we make this same decision to come. We don't have to come to worship.
In fact, many Christians do not. How odd it is that so many churches
may have a membership of 500 and only 220 gather for worship on
Sunday morning. Many are choosing not to come. They are deciding not
to turn away from the world and turn to the cross. Many of us notice that
people are choosing other forms of cultural worship on Saturday after-
noons or Sunday mornings. Driving to worship on Sunday mornings we
often see that other parking lots are more crowded with eager worshipers:
Home Depot, grocery stores, Sam's Club, soccer fields, and coffee shops.
Starbucks has become a place of worship for many people. The morning
paper has become sacred scriptures. A bagel and latte has become the
Communion meal. These are all substitutes for our supreme calling: to
worship the living God of the universe. When we choose to come

to worship, we are coming to a place that reminds us who we really are. It is a time of self-recognition and divine intervention.

There was a time in the United States when one could not shop on Sunday mornings and still be a strong Christian. Today such blue laws no longer exist. Today we find worship services on Saturday evening and Sunday evening to accommodate people who work on Sundays. But in our post-Christendom culture with Christianity becoming marginalized, we need to think about what our life in Christ means to us and to our communities. Worship and witness must be interwoven as a seamless whole. One of the most important commandments is the fourth, "Remember the Sabbath day by keeping it holy" (Ex 20:8). Choosing to honor the sabbath has become a signpost in a non-Christian culture.[6] In Exodus God adds an exclamation mark to the importance of the fourth commandment: "For six days, work is to be done, but the seventh day shall be your holy day, a day of sabbath rest to the LORD. Whoever does any work on it is to be put to death" (Ex 35:2). Coming to Jesus, seen here as resting from all work and coming to worship, is to be a rhythm of life, a pattern of returning again and again to Jesus and his body. Coming each week or (for some) each day represents repenting again and again. In so doing, we are turning away from other voices that are calling us, and we are listening to the true voice of our true Father in heaven. But repentance means more than just coming to worship.

The Christian life really entails an ongoing life of repentance and subsequent cleansing and empowerment. In fact, the whole Reformation in the sixteenth century centered on this question, which is foundational for the Christian life: What does it mean to repent (penance)? The medieval European church had decided that penance required our hard work to, in some way, earn God's favor. We must prove our heart is contrite. Martin Luther and the host of people who protested (thus they are Protestants) the authority of the Roman Catholic Curia to dispense grace subsequent to penance said, "No, repentance is a daily act. We must repent every day, over and over again." In fact, the iconic document of the Reformation, the Ninety-five Theses that Martin Luther nailed to the door of Wittenberg Chapel focused on the meaning of repentance. The Christian repents—turns away from self and then comes to Jesus—every day.

It is important to think specifically about what we are repenting from.

When we repent in a generic way, we are worshiping a generic "god." God, however, is not generic; he is specific and very personal. He has a name and he acts in history. Scripture does not talk about sin only in general ways. We read about pride or anger, but then Scripture gets very personal in the various sin lists[7] that leave us with little doubt. Sins are personal and they are corporate. Sins involve thoughts and actions. Sins are sometimes things we do to others and sometimes things we neglect to do for others. At different times and places, different sins become more of a problem. For the businessman with access to financial records, avarice (love of money) and tax evasion may be more of a temptation than for a fourteen-year-old on a football team. The temptations for a young woman going off to college differ from those of a grandmother living next door to her daughter. Some sins are more complex; they are systems of injustice, poverty, and prejudice.

Let me suggest some of the major cultural sins of the West in the twenty-first century. It seems, looking at newspapers, checking websites and media, and listening to conversations around us that we live in a consumerist, hypersexed, therapeutic, and violent society. We feel temptations to insulate ourselves from others, to entertain ourselves, and to "get even" all around us. Movies, video games, and postings on websites reveal all this. The internet is driven more by pornography than any other commodity. We need to name these temptations and be able to talk about them with each other. Then we must help each other repent of thoughts that lead to sinful behavior that leads us away from God, away from worship, and away from wholeness. We become what we are meant to be when we worship. The worshiping person is the complete person. Sin makes us less than we are meant to be. Sin drains us of both power and of love.

Temptation, sin, repentance. We need to repent over and over again, and that is OK. It is good and healthy to do so. Not only is God not surprised, it is what God expects of us. Repentance is our lifeline; worship is our response. It is good to become part of a repenting community. A repenting community is humble ("There, but by the grace of God, go I"). A repenting community easily forgives and supports. It is of little value to forgive repentant persons and then do nothing to support them in their quest for holiness. A person who comes with burdens and then repents needs prayer, encouragement, and discipleship.

A repenting community is a forgiving and a loving community. Each time we come to worship we are aware that the people around us share our struggles as well as our victories. Most of all, we belong to a community of people being made new into the image of Christ. This movement of re-creation occurs through the lifeline of repentance and thanksgiving. Thus, when we say that "come" is the first movement of the embodied life of the church, we mean that it is both a once-for-all-of-time event, and it is a way of life. Thus, self-emptying becomes a supreme virtue.

COMING TO CHURCH, COMING TO THE CROSS

One Sunday morning Nancy and I were singing praise songs in our church. The church was located in a community that had a high rate of poverty (over one-third of the population) and a very high rate of unemployment among men between the ages of eighteen and forty (over 60 percent). Once a paragon of industrial wealth, this community was now struggling to attract businesses and property owners. As we stood singing, looking up at the words on the screen, a man slowly walked up the isle on crutches and stood in front of us. He hummed with the songs, but didn't seem to be reading the words or actually singing. He seemed deep in thought. We moved in, and he sat next to us.

By the end of the service it was clear that he was a visitor and was also illiterate. We came up to him after the benediction and told him we have a time of fellowship after the service, and so we led him back to the fellowship hall to get to know him and to tell him about the church. It quickly became clear that this was not only his first time to our church, but it was his first time to church in decades (if he had ever attended at all). "Bob" said that he had spent the past year in a halfway house just two blocks away. After struggling with alcoholism for three decades, he woke up this morning and God said to him to go to church. He walked out the front door and saw our cross and walked in to worship. I asked him if he was a Christian, and his response was amazing: "Yes, that is what I want! I want to be a Christian."

And so Bob repented of his sin, confessed Jesus, and then was baptized. He became part of a family. Church members brought him food, visited him at the halfway house, helped him get his own apartment, and brought him cassettes of the Gospels (remember cassettes?) for him to listen to. Slowly he learned to read, and he proudly wore reading glasses to show he was learning to read the Bible. When we come to the cross, we come to a community of people at the foot of the cross. Conversion introduces us to a community. We find that we are not alone.

It is a great gift that God gives us in that our coming to the cross is coming to a community of people who, like us, are commanded to love each other. We come to a loving community. Salvation is found in a community called the "body of Christ." Even in the early church, families were baptized together, and Christians were identified as the "church in Ephesus," the "church in Philippi."[8] Of course, for many people the local church they attend (as if the Christian life is a show or entertainment event) bothers them. They don't like the people or they find certain leaders irritating. And yet, we need to put our irritations and personal peeves in perspective. Let me do so with three perspectives about the church as a community of sinners.

First, we see the value of the church as a community (the body of Christ) in the rhythms and passages of life. Recently a good friend's wife died of cancer. She was in the prime of her life. They just bought a new home, and they took a year remodeling the kitchen, repainting the walls, redoing the bathroom, and buying some new furniture that fit in beautifully. They were set, as a couple with children now grown, to develop more of a ministry of hospitality. Her radiation treatments proved inadequate, and the cancer returned with a vengeance just as they were finishing the house. He had been promoted in his work and was doing very well, and then all of his life seemed to be mocked with the sudden death of his wife. He was all alone. But he was not all alone. As a Christian, the local church had a prayer service for his wife as she was suffering. Hundreds came to pray and to support the family. Upon her death they held a beautiful memorial service. There was food, music, crying, and storytelling. Then there were the meals. As my friend said two months later, "I haven't been able to cook a thing except for some coffee. My refrigerator is still full." Alone, but in community with social, physical, and spiritual needs being met.

The same happens with weddings and births for the person who has come to the cross. The Christian lives in a community that cares about and helps to carry the person through transitions in life. A Christian getting married in a church has the church to support the wedding itself and then to help nurture the marriage. Marriage and raising children can be very difficult. God has so designed the church to be a place where family life and singleness are held, protected, and supported. Community life helps to bear the burdens and heal the wounds that we inflict on those we love. When a child is born, church members can (or at least should) come alongside to provide meals and baby clothes and to intercede for the family. How wonderful it is to have a blessed community in which to grow, develop, suffer, and rejoice. We are not alone when we come to Christ.

A second perspective on the communal nature of Christian life comes from comparing it with other religions. My family lived for eight years in Southeast Asia amid Muslims, Sikhs, Buddhists, Hindus, "Chinese religionists,"[9] and Christians. We have visited more temples and mosques than our children wanted to, but in doing so we learned a lot. Almost all religions may have a social element, but in general, salvation and piety is radically individual. Individuals go to a Buddhist temple alone (or with some family members) to light joss sticks, bring offerings, or carry out other acts of piety. There is no religious service where everyone gathers together. Even on sacred days, individuals come and go as they please. Some temples are like ancient Near Eastern temples where the sacrifices become items to eat. Temples were like markets and restaurants combined. It is a very different type of piety. The church must be a place of gathering in community, of listening to each other, of caring for others. When we come to the cross we find out that there are a lot of people at the foot of the cross. We are not alone. Christian faith is communal from start to finish—even for eternity. Heaven is a city, a banquet, a house, not a private cave. Heaven is a place of communal resurrected life. How wonderful, really.

The third perspective is essentially a new concern for the church in the West. I put it this way: any local church must reflect its local, particular context, but it must also be a place for ethnic minorities (or diverse groups) to find home as a cultural group. A local church includes every person and every people group. This is the connected and contextual concern of the church revealed in a new way. People coming to a local church should all be welcomed! All languages, nationalities, and ethnicities should be welcome. The church should reflect where we are going—heaven is a vastly multicultural place:

> After this I looked, and there before me was a great multitude that no one could count, from every nation, tribe, people and language, standing before the throne and before the Lamb. (Rev 7:9)

God loves cultural diversity. He absolutely loves it! God also loves clear and truthful communication, and communication is cultural. Some cultures are so different, and some people are so marginalized and oppressed that local churches need to make room for these groups to gather together, sing in their own language, and have a culturally appropriate witness to their own people.

I worshiped one evening with a mostly African American gathering in the East End of Pittsburgh. The preaching was good, the music was great, but the service was sort of dragging, and the leadership either wanted to leave, or they were waiting for someone to come. They were all looking at the back door. Then, after about ninety minutes, slowly the back door opened and in walked about ten visitors: the worship group from a new local church in the city, Hosanna Church. It was a newer church made up of ethnic Nepalese from Bhutan. They slowly walked forward, sat on the floor with their stringed instruments and percussion instruments, and began to sing rhythmic praise songs in Nepali. The African Americans loved the music, but we did not understand the words. We had to have summaries of all the lyrics after each song. It was a great image or signpost of the kingdom of heaven for this city. However, we could not worship like this all the time unless all in the local congregation learned Nepali. Even then, our outreach to Nepalese would have been greatly curtailed if we insisted that they worship with us each week; we would overwhelm their much smaller community. With their own worship songs and familiar language, new immigrants feel very much at home and loved. Every person should gather together, and every ethnic group needs a home. This concern for witness, I believe, is very important as we think about coming together.

Timothy Schultz tells an interesting story of a Hindu family who had migrated from India to New Jersey.[10] Schultz and others befriended this particular family. One evening, the father, Ketan, quietly said that he was overwhelmed with problems. As is true for all of us, many of his problems were of his own doing. Timothy simply told him that Jesus would forgive every one of his sins. It was nothing complicated, but it was exactly what he needed to hear about the God who created him: he would forgive him. Ketan came to faith, began to read his Bible and, with other family members and friends, started a little prayer group. Things seemed to be going well, but one thing was missing. Out of pain and great humility, Timothy admits his own responsibility with the sudden decline of the small Indian Christian movement. "First, we failed to create a consistent and contextualized experience of Christ *bhakti*, or worship of Christ for Ketan, his family, and the Hindu community that was involved in this brief gospel movement."[11] When we come together, we need to recognize both the all-inclusive kingdom and the each-and-every-nation nature of the kingdom of God. Multicultural does not mean all cultures are always together. That often drowns out the gifts and voices of smaller cultural groups. The church is contextual. We come together as a multicultural community and as a cultural family.

COME TO WORSHIP!

I have an image from years ago when I was at a conference in South Africa. It was Sunday morning and a group of international mission scholars were going to worship. On the way, we stopped at an intersection waiting for the light to change. Walking slowly to our right on the side of the road was a group of thirty or forty local women, all dressed in uniform, singing, swaying, and clapping. They exuded a great deal of joy and expectation as they, oblivious to their surroundings, seemed to be sliding or emerging into church rather than just going to church. Worship was the way of coming to church. Worship seemed to carry them along until they arrived for a much more robust time of worship. I have often thought that this is a great image or even ideal for what we read in the Psalms:

> Make a joyful noise to the LORD, all the earth.
>> Worship the LORD with gladness;
>> Come into his presence with singing . . .
> Enter his gates with thanksgiving,
>> And his courts with praise!
>> Give thanks to him, bless his name. (Ps 100:1-2, 4 NRSV)

Psalm 100 describes worshipers coming in an attitude and a life of praise. The book of Psalms also contains fifteen Psalms of Ascent (Ps 120–134), which are understood to have been sung as the Israelites came to Jerusalem to worship. Coming *to* worship may actually involve coming *as* we worship.

As a reminder, the church has two basic purposes, not three, not four, and not one. God has called together the church for worship and witness. Matthew 28 as well as Acts 2 are foundational in this regard.

> When they saw him, they worshiped him; but some doubted. Then Jesus came to them and said, "All authority in heaven and on earth has been given to me. Therefore go and make disciples of all nations." (Mt 28:17-19)

It is in the context of worship (the natural and normal response to being in the presence of the living God) that Jesus gives the command. The command is to make disciples of all nations. The command is not

first to teach (although that is subsumed under making disciples), nor is
the command to baptize (although that is also part of making disciples).
In Acts we find something very similar. Jesus gives the basic command
for the disciples in Acts 1:8, the foundational purpose ("You will be my
witnesses"), and then in Acts 2 the Holy Spirit comes during prayer and
Peter gives a call to repent and follow Jesus.

These two purposes are, in this book and in the Church's life, given as
the beginning and the end of worship. Worship begins with "come" and
it ends with "go!" A church that worships poorly will have a poor witness.
A church that has little or no witness is not focused on Jesus who is the
Savior of the world. Worship is the main reason we gather together
because when we worship together we are most fully alive and most fully
being healed and reconciled. There is no such thing as reconciliation
without Christ. Relationships have hope in the presence of Jesus Christ,
and healing is at hand in the midst of worship.

I first learned in Asia something about healing services and exorcism.
I am not an exorcist myself, but I have great respect for people who have
this ministry. A healing service or service of exorcism always starts with
worship of God. We begin with prayer, prayers of confession and repentance to make sure we are right before God, and prayers for God's
presence. "Come, Holy Spirit!" Then we often sing hymns and spiritual
songs, making the room a room of worship. It is in the midst of worship
that the demons are cast out or that prayers for healing begin. Mission[12]
belongs with worship, and worship must always flow into witness. We
will bring this topic up again in chapter five when we talk about "go!"
Here we want to understand what worship has to do with "come!" We
come, not so much to a place, but to an existence: a "place" that is filled
with the presence of the creator and the healing God. The God of history
and the God of the future is here, now. When we come, we are coming
into this divine environment, a type of existence that Moses experienced
ascending the mountain, Elijah experienced with the prophets of Baal,
and Saul on the road to Damascus.

So as its foundation, worship has memory. One of the early saints,
Mark the Ascetic, wrote a letter to a younger disciple about how to live

the Christian life. It seems that Nicolas had become concerned about temptations, including carnal desires and anger. Mark is clear that the whole Christian life begins with proper memory, remembering what we are thankful for.

> This my son, is how you should begin your life according to God. You should continually and unceasingly call to mind all the blessings which God in his Love has bestowed upon you in the past, and still bestows for the salvation of your soul. You must not let forgetfulness of evil or laziness make you grow unmindful of these many great blessings and so pass the rest of your life uselessly and ungratefully. . . . Thus, the soul recalls the blessings of God's love.[13]

Worship begins with thanksgiving, and thanksgiving requires us to remember. Thus, the foundation of worship is to recall all that God has done for us, both in Christ Jesus as what is foundational for all people and specifically what he has done in your life. We need to remember our conversion, our baptism, how God has protected and guided us. Worship begins with thanksgiving. And you can't thank unless you remember.

COME TO THINK OF IT . . .

Come to think of it, the fullness of the church depends on this foundational movement in worship: come. Although some churches have made conversion the main or only element of worship (testimonies), most churches do not celebrate the remarkable transformation that takes place in conversion. Scripture describes the importance of conversion, the turning of one person to follow Jesus, as an event of cosmic proportions. We are far too unimpressed. God is like a prodigal father, one who gives overabundantly to his children. He is one who stands at the edge of heaven preoccupied with the lost, lonely, and unloved, ready to greet them home and to shower them (us) with great gifts of joy. God's posture is leaning toward us.

We should be more like the angels and celebrate each homecoming, each person who says simply, "I can't do it. Help me, Jesus." Luke 15, the great chapter on lost things, pictures God as a shepherd, a woman in a household, and a waiting father. Each case depicts God as almost anxiously seeking what is lost. God is not sitting in a warm cabin hoping the daughter will find her way back to the warmth of the fireplace. God is the active seeker. God is the one who finds, and we are the hopeless ones who are lost.

> Or suppose a woman has ten silver coins and loses one. Doesn't she light a lamp, sweep the house and search carefully until she finds it? And when she finds it, she calls her friends and neighbors together and says, "Rejoice with me; I have found my lost coin." In the same way, I tell you, there is rejoicing in the presence of the angels of God over one sinner who repents. (Lk 15:8-10)

After each of the lost-and-found stories, there is joy and celebration of cosmic proportions. "I tell you that in the same way there will be more rejoicing in heaven over one sinner who repents than over ninety-nine righteous persons who do not need to repent" (Lk 15:7).

One of my most memorable times of worship took place in an intimate group of about 18,000 at a missionary convention in Urbana, Illinois. The music that called us to worship underscored the relationship of conversion to the meaning of the church.

> Come, now is the time to worship
> Come, now is the time to give your heart
> Come, just as you are, to worship.
> Come, just as you are, before your God
> Come
> One day every tongue will confess, "You are God"
> One day every knee will bow
> Still the greatest treasure remains for those
> Who gladly choose you now[14]

This song of coming to worship expresses so clearly what it means to live into the first body movement of the church, come: "Give your heart . . . just as you are . . . every tongue will confess . . . greatest treasure."

The church is a place where people are called and where they become new people: sons and daughters of the living God. They give their life (symbolized as the heart) to God, and this is their worship. Coming to God with no "ifs, ands, or buts" is true worship. And, as the song above makes clear, there is a close relationship between this individual coming to worship and all of the nations coming to worship. In my coming to worship, in your turning to Christ, we are getting a glimpse of heaven with the nations coming to worship Jesus. As the Church, we look forward, with hope, to all the nations around the throne. We must always see our particular coming to God as our part in the great stream of nations coming to the Lord's House.

> In the last days
>   the mountain of the LORD's temple will be established
>   as the highest of the mountains;
>   it will be exalted above the hills,
>   and all nations will stream to it.
> Many peoples will come and say,
>   "Come, let us go up to the mountain of the LORD,
>   to the temple of the God of Jacob.
>   He will teach us his ways,
>   so that we may walk in his paths." (Is 2:2-3)

Conversion naturally leads to heavenly and earthly praise, and this will flow into the call of all peoples to come together as reconciled nations. But we are getting ahead of ourselves. We started this chapter with a story of a fraternity student coming to read about Jesus and his life being completely transformed. The Church, each local church as well, is made up of little miracles walking around—people who were self-centered, powerless, and lost. Each person represents a miracle of God's grace, and each person now has the Spirit of the living God dwelling in him or her. We may not see this all the time, but we must remember who we are dealing with in the church. Church members—converted and baptized individuals—are now people with the power of the living God as they participate in God's transforming life for themselves, and through them for their own church and community. This is cause for great celebration. We should be filled with awe and praise, and so we stand. And so, now that we have "come" to church, we embrace the next body movement: We stand in praise.

4

STAND

Enter his gates with thanksgiving,
and his courts with praise!

PSALM 100:4

I REMEMBER VERY CLEARLY THE FIRST TIME I attended a worship service in South Africa. The time of praise was delightful, joyous, uniting, and moving. I guess I expected this to be the case, but what I was not prepared for was the offering. When it was announced that we would have a time of offering everyone (except for me) spontaneously sprang to their feet and began clapping and singing; hands, feet, and mouths moved in rhythmic praise. Then, row by row, everyone processed to the front to joyously put their offering in a large basket. It was a time of praise and celebration, with not a little dancing. Giving was a time of praise. Praise has a certain joy and force to it that often causes us to lift our hands and move our feet. It is appropriate to stand when we praise, and it is appropriate to enter worship time together with praise.

But such praise is not just an African expression. I have been in worship in China, and I have also seen some remarkable films of worship in house churches in China where everyone is smiling, clapping, and shouting songs of praise. The energy and joy comes across even when I don't understand a word of the songs. I have also had the opportunity to worship on Easter Sunday at the Almudena Cathedral in Madrid, Spain. There was not as much dancing, but there was great joy, as over a thousand people stood singing praise with a large pipe organ leading the way. Praising God is a Spirit-infused activity that we enter into as if entering the very Holy of Holies. Praise is a response, but it is also a transformation of us and our community, as we will discover.

Worship, especially praise, should be an easy and joyous experience for people to enter into. There should be a joyous, even at times reckless, plunge into praise. It is a thoughtful emotional response to God—because God is so, so good, and so remarkably loving.

Praise is the way we enter worship together; in fact, it is a good way to always enter into God's presence, whether to pray with a friend, in a corporate worship service, or in private prayer. However, praise is not just rational, as if to say, "God has done this, so I should say this." Absolutely not. Being very emotional, praise involves our whole being. Stoic praise is foreign to the Bible and to Christian worship, through the ages and across the nations. Praise involves drawing near to the triune God of the universe whose name is love, whose touch saves and heals, and whose breath gives life. By the time you finish this chapter I hope you will be led into deeper and more profound worship, even as you think new thoughts. Mind and heart, ideas and feelings, intimacy and ecstasy should grow together and overflow into joyful praise.

PRAISE IS AS PRAISE DOES

The first part of every worship service, the first element in coming to church, the first and eternal work we are called to is praise.

Human history, on one level, is the story of humanity's constant turn toward self and personal or cultural idolatry. Wars are mostly about one

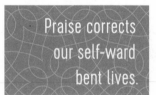
Praise corrects our self-ward bent lives.

person (or nation) dominating others, which becomes a conquest for power or for control of trade or resources or money. Family conflict often tells a story of lack of appreciation for the other and the need for affirmation. We look after ourselves so much that our lives often turn into self-centered narratives. This is life centered on ourselves or on our people.

Praise moves us in the other direction. Praise corrects our orientation and reminds us of who we really are. In praise, Jesus sits on the throne and all the nations bow down before him. This image (from Rev 7) shows us a corrective. Our basic identity does not derive from what we produce, what we do as a job, who we are in our family, or even who we are as a people. All around that throne, on the same level ground, are people of every tribe and people and nation, people of every profession, every ability, and those with very limited ability. Every tribe, every family, every individual is valued because of their praise of the One in whose image we are fashioned. Praise not only corrects us, it also heals broken hearts, reconciles enemies, brings forgiveness, and helps in our being remade in the image of God. Praise is amazing!

I think the strongest impression we had of the thirty-five different churches we visited in 2013 was that of praise. Most newer churches—and many older churches—had a time of praise and prayer at the beginning of the service. Praise of the God of the universe is more than singing, however, but it is certainly not less. When students from the United States visit Christians in Africa, Latin America, or Asia, they inevitably talk about the engaging, fully embodied worship. Dancing, drumming, singing, clapping, raising hands, and even shouts of praise are part of global worship today. More praise music is written in more languages today than ever in the history of the church. Songs of praise, in Portuguese, Chinese, Kachin, Korean, Bahasa Malaysia, Arabic, and even English are flooding the global church today in joyous songs and choruses.

Before we look more closely at what Christian praise is, I think it is helpful to step back for a moment and reflect on how our larger topic of worship functions globally and historically. One of the great lessons that has stuck with me in the study of history of religions is the role of worship for a nation or a people. Throughout history and across cultures, worship orients a people or gives a people identity: values and an identity that are reinforced through ritual. But this worship by a particular people creates identity in such a way that they begin to be shaped into the image of that which they worship. The ancient Celts ruled from the British Isles, but for a period of about four centuries the Celts dominated much of western Europe (before the time of Christ). The Celts were a warrior people who conquered even as far as Galatia in modern-day Turkey.

It is fitting that one of the main gods of the Celts was Lugh (also Lug) who was a warrior, a shining "one with long arms or hands." He had a magic fiery spear and a protective shield. Worshiping and praising a warrior god helped to shape Celtic culture into a warrior nation—in the image of the god they worshiped.

Other cultures or nations have had gods or goddesses of love, of wine, or of fertility. One can guess that such deities shaped cultures and individuals. Today much of Western culture has  moved away from traditional worship. An almost ritualistic preoccupation with material goods, games of violence, and sexually explicit content has made these into idols that draw us into ritualistic practices and reinforce an identity that reflects what we worship. This is the negative side of worship, and it is all around us, calling us to come and adore what we have made.

Speaking more positively, when we come to worship in a Christian church and begin in praise, we are reminding ourselves of who we are. We are God's creation, made in his image—an image that has become tarnished and damaged, but which worship helps to restore.

We are who we are because of who God is. God gives our lives meaning and purpose, wholeness and health. In this sense, praise serves as a corrective and a reminder. Praise, built upon thanksgiving, provides the foundation of worship. But what exactly is praise?

WHAT IS PRAISE?

When traveling in Asia I often visit temples and mosques and other sacred places. In fact, when we lived in Singapore we would often walk past a very old sacred Bodhi tree. We knew it was considered sacred because people would come and light joss sticks and candles. They would also place small sacred statues or fetishes in the tree. In Buddhist temples people would come also to light joss sticks in front of an image of the Buddha or of the Goddess of Mercy, Guan Yin. In Singapore (a fairly affluent country) when I asked adults why they were washing the Buddha or lighting joss sticks, it was often for a good business deal or for their children to do well on their exams. They were hoping to influence fate by their devotion. In Myanmar (a very poor country), when I asked the same question, adults would often say it was for good health or for more food or medicine. The needs were more basic, but the practice worked from the same understanding: they hoped that through their devotion they might have a better life.

This is a type of worship, but it is not praise. The various "health and wealth" gospels proliferating today are really no different. These types of worship focus not on what God (or Buddha, or an idol, or a god or goddess) has already done for us. Such worship comes on the other side of a god's action. It is trying to get the god or idol or ancestor to act for us. Christian praise is very different.

Christian praise is a response to what God has already done.

Thus, Christian worship begins in praise because God, the holy God of the universe, has already acted and continues to give life and grace and mercy every day. Our praise wells up in response from the other side of God's action. This is very significant. Worship in most all religions of the world is an effort to get a god or idol to act. But Christian praise is our response to God's being and to his action already completed. This means that the foundation of our praise is remembering. Memory forms the foundation of praise, and praise and thanksgiving form the foundation of worship. Scripture is replete with examples of how important it is to remember what God has done. We will look at some of these Scriptures later, but remember that Israel's forgetfulness was the reason for their exile and judgment from God. It makes you think, doesn't it? Yes, remember Israel's forgetfulness.

At this point we need to think about memory. A few phrases guide my life, and most of those close to me hear me say them quite often. One of those phrases states, "Jesus is on the throne." It is a good short sentence to reassure us when we begin to doubt or when life is difficult. Jesus is still on the throne and he rules over all. Another expression I use almost every day is, "History is very important." And it is. So many times I find that remembering what has happened or finding out what others have remembered about an event or experience helps to explain what people think, write, do, or feel. Remembering that Jesus is on the throne encourages us when things don't seem to be going well. It may not appear that God cares, but remembering that he rules from on high and (at the same time) that he is the Good Shepherd helps us to carry on. These are true statements that ground our existence. So our praise requires that we remember some important truths. We need to remember:

- Praise has a subject.
- We praise God for who God is.
- We praise God for what he has done.
- We praise God for what he has done for me.
- We praise God for what he will do.

PRAISE HAS A SUBJECT

I have always found it rather odd to be at an American Thanksgiving dinner with a family that is atheistic or that has stopped going to church. We will talk about what we are thankful for at the table, but whom are we thanking? Thanksgiving is always directed to the one who has provided or protected. When we enter a time of thanksgiving and praise, we are entering into the presence of the One who identified himself to Moses as "I AM" (Ex 3:14). God, known as YHWH in the Old Testament, is the one who exists before everything and everyone else. God is the one to whom all else owes its existence. A child should be very thankful for the mother who brought her into this world, who fed her, and who cared for her until she could care for herself. But all of existence, even that little child and her mother, owes everything to God. Only by God's power and wisdom does anything exist. Therefore, our praise is not general or free-floating praise. Our praise is a response to God who, in all things, takes the initiative in our lives. We live our lives in response to God: who he is and what God has done.

On a very human level we heap praise on a hero, great athlete, or movie star—both corporately and individually. We are designed to praise, the question is who or what group do we praise? Having played a lot of sports and having attended many major college and professional sporting events, I can say from semi-empirical data that people love to praise. We love to praise the single hero who hits the grand slam at the bottom of the ninth inning, and we like to praise the basketball team when they run out to "take the court" at the completion of the National Anthem. A hockey arena will erupt in praise—15,000 people on their feet—when a goal is scored. A natatorium will echo with shouts when a school or national record is broken in the 100 meter freestyle. We don't praise in general. We praise the memory of greatness when a retired Hall of Fame player comes out at halftime. We praise a specific team for their greatness, and we shout and praise in hope when a team comes out for the second half of a basketball game when the score is tied.

Yes, praise has a subject. The subject (God, athlete, rock star) elicits the praise. In fact, the subject is what makes praise meaningful and truthful.

However, false praise, like false worship, makes us less fully human. But worship of the triune God, the creator of the universe in whose image we are fashioned—this worship makes us more fully who we are meant to be. It helps to correct us, to clean us, to remake us in wonderful ways. Praise leads to our transformation. For this reason it is important to grow in our knowledge of God: so that our worship can be more meaningful, accurate, joyful, and fulfilling.

Our praise is more than a thank you, but it is a thank you. Our praise says something like, "Oh, my . . . oh, oh, oh, my. So awesome and wonderful! I cannot believe . . . I cannot even . . . I don't have words for this. God, you are so remarkable, beautiful, good, and compassionate. Oh, oh my, I don't know what to say! Unbelievable. Thank you, Father, Son, and Holy Spirit. I praise you, I want all of creation and all nations to know how great you are." And that is just the beginning. Praise is the response to being in God's presence. The deeper, the more informed, and the more humble our approach to God, the more we want to express to God and to all of the nations and even to creation our response of praise.

So where do we go to raise our vision of God to deepen our praise? Praise deepens and is vitalized through greater and greater knowledge of

Scripture. Reading broadly in Scripture and meditating deeply on passages increases our praise and deepens our own lives. Why do I say it deepens our own lives? Because the more we know about God through Scripture, the more we realize that God, the triune God of all creation and all time is both mighty and intimate, both magnificent and personal, both frightening and gentle. Praise overflows from greater understanding of God in Scripture. Reading about God's encounter with Moses in the burning bush (Ex 3) and then his appearance with Moses on the mountain reveals his magnificence, something of his mystery (the bush did not burn up) and his desires for us. Looking at various appearances of God communicates something of his nature (including his thoughts) to us. "Don't worship other Gods" is pretty clear, and it helps us to be loyal. "Don't covet your neighbor's wife" also tells us that God cares about fidelity and loyalty. "Don't bear false witness" (or just "Don't lie") tells us that God cares about loyalty to what is true. Knowing more about God, his ways, and his wonders gives our praise vitality.

We turn now to the reasons for praising God. This is not meant to be a checklist to take to worship next week. That would be fairly disruptive, and it would work against everything that praise is meant to be: our full response to God, which is not merely a rational, carefully reasoned critical engagement with God. Nonetheless, we need to think about the reasons for praising God because many times churches, families, or individuals get trapped in a narrow view of God or of praise of God. *Worship is mindful, not mindless.*

Thus, look at these reasons and then take time yourself to meditate on the greatness and goodness of God.

PRAISE FOR WHO GOD IS

Most importantly and foundationally we come to worship to praise God for who God is. God is awesome. God is beautiful. God is powerful. God is gentle and kind. God is attentive. Of course, God is much more than these abstract nouns, but before God does anything at all, God is worthy of our praise. Indigenous peoples in North America worship "Creator." When the gospel was first proclaimed in nearly every region, the people had a belief and great respect for Creator. Indigenous people know about Creator from creation. Creation points to the Creator, and so they worshiped Creator before they knew (through the Great Spirit) about the Creator's Son.

We begin our worship (as we might begin in any loving relationship) just praising the other person for who they are, not for what they have done for me. God is worthy of all our praise and all of our devotion. Here are some Scriptures that remind us of who God is:

> For great is the LORD and most worthy of praise;
> He is to be feared above all gods. (Ps 96:4)

> Great is the LORD and most worthy of praise;
> his greatness no one can fathom. (Ps 145:3)

> "'Holy, holy, holy,
> is the Lord God Almighty,'
> who was, and is, and is to come. (Rev 4:8)

> "You are worthy, our Lord and God,
> to receive glory and honor and power,
> for you created all things,
> and by your will they were created
> and have their being." (Rev 4:11)

Praising God for who God is summarizes God's character and God's work together. This means that we praise God for characteristics—being true, holy, powerful, just, kind—but these characteristics are really summaries of what God has done. Think of this in human terms. When someone asks about my wife, and I say she is very kind and remarkably discerning (both of which are true), I can say this because I have seen her do very kind things to some not-so-kind people, and I have heard others thank me for her discernment in giving advice.

When we praise God for being a loving God, we are not just quoting 1 John 4:8, but we are summarizing God's work through time. Abstract nouns about God's character become foundational words in our praise. Here are some classic lines from hymns and some newer lines from more recent praise songs:

Great Is Thy Faithfulness
Great is Thy faithfulness, O God my Father,
There is no shadow of turning with Thee;
Thou changest not, Thy compassions they fail not;
As Thou hast been, Thou forever wilt be.
Great is Thy faithfulness! Great is Thy faithfulness!
Morning by morning new mercies I see;
All I have needed Thy had hath provided;
Great is Thy faithfulness, Lord unto me![1]

Holy Is the Lord
We stand and lift up our hands
For the joy of the Lord is our strength
We bow down and worship Him now
How great, how awesome is He
And together we sing . . .
[Chorus]
Holy is the Lord God Almighty
The earth is filled with His glory
Holy is the Lord God Almighty
The earth is filled with His glory
The earth is filled with His glory[2]

Many hymns, psalms, and other spiritual songs and poetry praise God
for who God is. But most all of these poems of praise cannot stop with
general praise for the character of God. Most of them quickly cross the
artificial divide from praise for who God is to praise and thanksgiving
for what God has done. Who God is (his character) is really just a
summary of God's attributes in harmony with God's actions.

PRAISE FOR WHAT GOD HAS DONE

I want to return to the great contrast between Christian worship and
praise and the worship of most religions in the world. I don't think
Christians realize how beautiful it is that God does not need to be
prodded into acting on our behalf. Most of the sacred places our family
encountered in Asia had an idol, god, or goddess who was to be honored
by those who sought the favor or help of the deity. Bringing sacrifices of

food or other types of devotion was necessary to bring the particular blessings of each deity. Guan Yin, the Goddess of Mercy, is an important goddess among the Chinese, who believe she brings mercy and salvation to the devotee. Sarasvati is a goddess of learning, the arts, and music. In spring there is a special day to honor her (Vasant Panchami), and parents who wish their children to do well in school—especially learning their alphabet—will make their appeal to Sarasvati. Thousands of deities in Asia are appealed to for help in this world or to escape this world. In contrast, our worship begins with praise because God has already acted on our behalf. If God had not already acted, we would start our worship (as do many Asian religions) trying to wake God up to act for us, or we would offer food, or we might make other appeals to God to do something.

No, Christian worship is different from worship in Hindu or Sikh temples or Buddhist wats. God has done great things, and so when we come into his presence, our worship begins with praise. The Old Testament gives evidence of this. So what exactly has God done?

In Old Testament Scriptures we find eighty-seven references to God being the one who delivered the Israelites from Egypt. Sometimes it is a retelling of the story, sometimes it is a reminder to pass on this story to children and grandchildren, but often it is simply a way of identifying God. "Oh, you are worshiping that God, the one who liberated people from slavery!" In the preface to the Ten Commandments, God says to Moses, "I am the LORD your God, who brought you out of Egypt, out of the land of slavery" (Ex 20:2). Two of the main works of God for Israel are national liberation and the gift of knowing how to live (the Law). God has freed (or saved) his people and then set them on the right path.

One of the most common words in the Old Testament is remember (zakar). Israel is constantly told to remember what God has done for them. But think about this: In remembering what God has done, they remember who they are. They are a people who have been saved and have been given a purpose. In fact, at times they are told specifically to remember and to praise. Remembrance and praise go together. Leviticus

commands the Israelites to keep various festivals, one of which is the
festival of booths. It is a little bit like camping out for a week.

> Celebrate this as a festival to the LORD for seven days each year. . . . Live in
> temporary shelters for seven days: All native-born Israelites are to live in such
> shelters so your descendants will know that I had the Israelites live in tem-
> porary shelters when I brought them out of Egypt. I am the LORD your God.
> (Lev 23:41-43)

In other words, remember who you are and whence you came.

This is all true of Israel, but it is only the beginning for Christian
worship. As Christians we praise God for what God has done through
Jesus Christ. Again, we are remembering history, which leads us to praise.

Jesus was born a miraculous birth to a virgin! Praise the Lord.

Jesus identified with us fully in birth and baptism! Praise the Lord.

Jesus called people and taught them! Praise the Lord.

Jesus touched people and healed them! Praise the Lord.

Jesus taught us how to live faithfully! Praise the Lord.

Jesus was glorified on a mountain! Praise the Lord.

Jesus said he was going to die for us—and he did. Praise the Lord.

Jesus gave us a mission to continue his work! Praise the Lord.

Jesus sent his Holy Spirit to guide and protect us! Praise the Lord.

Of course, we can praise God for much else that he has done for us in
Jesus Christ. This brief list begins to show how deep and wide the work
is that God has done for us. We need to remember what God has done—
all that God has done—so that our praise is rich and ever flowing in new
songs of joyous praise.

But the work that God has done did not end with Jesus' life, death, and
resurrection. His ascension means that his work continues, as he inter-
cedes for us, in our lives and the lives of those around us. This also leads
us to praise.

PRAISE FOR WHAT GOD HAS DONE FOR ME/US

As a younger Christian I was often confused about the difference between
thanksgiving and praise. I learned, as many of us have, that we should

pray according the acronym ACTS: Adoration, Confession, Thanksgiving, and Supplication.[3] It is easy to remember, but I have never found it very helpful. I have found it more helpful to let go of my anxiety concerning the difference between adoration (praise) and thanksgiving. Both are a response to God for what God has already done for us. However, we do not just praise God for abstract nouns (love, mercy, etc.). Nor do we only thank God for the cosmic and universal work that God has done. We also praise God for how those nouns—which describe his very character—have touched us personally. The triune God is not just far off and awesome. He is also intimate, personal, and gentle. He has actually touched me to save me as a person in a family, a community, and a culture. I thank God for saving my daughter from a terrible fall and for bringing my neighbor to faith in Christ.

Both the Psalms and Paul's letters actually command us to remember and to thank God for what he has done. Psalm 40 expresses this type of praise as rooted in David's telling history of what God has done for him (that is, his testimony). Then after reflecting on how God has personally been his savior and help so many times, he says the following:

Many, LORD my God,
    are the wonders you have done,
    the things you planned for us.
None can compare with you;
    were I to speak and tell of your deeds,
    they would be too many to declare. (Ps 40:5)

In Psalm 59, David gets more specific in his praise for God. He is thankful that God has helped him escape from Saul. After recounting how God protected him, he goes into praise: "But I will sing of your strength, in the morning I will sing of your love. . . . You are my strength, I sing praise to you" (Ps 59:16-17).

These psalms provide antecedents for the nineteenth-century hymn "Count your blessings, name them one by one." We should count our blessings. Mark them. Say them out loud. But more than that, in Psalm 40 and other psalms, we are also to give a testimony to others of what God has done for us. Such a testimony, whether one of salvation from sin or of God's provision and presence in difficult times, all end in praise. That is right: *Testimonies are acts of praise.*

I have listened to hundreds of personal testimonies in worship services, college fellowship groups, and evangelism classes in seminaries. In all these testimonies I have never heard someone end by claiming it was their own wisdom that helped them figure out God or who claimed anything of themselves. In fact, all testimonies end with some expression about how one's life has been changed by God's divine intervention. Finally, all testimonies end as verbal acts of praise.

Because of this, I strongly recommend recovering the place of testimony in our worship. As Psalm 40 expresses it,

> I proclaim your saving acts in the great assembly;
> I do not seal my lips, LORD,
> as you know.
> I do not hide your righteousness in my heart;
> I speak of your faithfulness and your saving help.
> I do not conceal your love and your faithfulness
> from the great assembly. (Ps 40:9-10)

According to King David in this prayer, it would be an act of disobedience if one were to keep her or his mouth shut about what God has done. It is an act of faithfulness and obedience to tell "in the great congregation" what God has done for you. Such testimonies help us all in our praise.

Nancy and I were visiting a large new church in Los Angeles where most of the people were in their twenties (some as old as thirty-five) and were from many different cultural backgrounds. The music was very professional, with the usual guitars, keyboard, drums, and vocalists. After some time of praise, the pastor announced that Mary, a local drama student at a large university, was going to give a testimony. Mary came forward and sat, talk-show like, on a stool holding the microphone. She proceeded to tell an amazing story. The professor of an introductory acting class asked all the students to prepare to present "something extreme" to the class. Having been an adolescent once myself, I know that this was a very unwise assignment. You don't need to tell adolescents to do something extreme; this is the very thing that gets them in trouble and often shortens their life span.

However, Mary decided that, as a Christian, she would write a hymn of love to Jesus and sing it in the class. A bold and extreme Christian witness in a secular university drama class. So, after a few weeks of presentations with only two students left to do their "extreme" presentation, Mary brought her guitar to class, and then Alice was called on as the second-to-last person to present. Mary would be last. Alice took a Bible (could it be, two Christians presenting as the last two students in the class?). Alice led the class out by a trashcan on campus and proceeded to slowly read portions of the Old Testament about commands to make war, God punishing the nations, sending Israel into exile, and then she read imprecatory Psalms: "Happy shall they be who take your little ones and dash them against the rock!" (Ps 137:9 NRSV). With each violent passage, Alice would say something like "Who could ever believe in a God like that? I don't believe in a God like this!" Then she would tear out the page from the Bible and burn it and drop the page in the trashcan. It was extreme drama.

This was the warm-up for Mary to sing her love song to Jesus. Back in the classroom she pulled out her guitar, said a brief prayer under her breath, and sang a love song to Jesus, expressing thanks for both his love and compassion for her. The class was silent and then all went home. All, that is, except for Alice. As Mary was packing up her guitar, Alice came forward with tears in her eyes. "That was beautiful. That is the God I want to know. Can you help me get to know Jesus?" And so, after a few days of Bible study and prayer, Alice gave her life to Christ.

On this particular Sunday, Mary expressed thanks to God for redeeming a difficult situation and bringing Alice to faith. The congregation was filled with praise and joy. Then, to add greater praise and thanksgiving, Mary said, "And Alice wanted to come to worship with me today to express her thanksgiving to Jesus. Alice, come up here with me." Sudden praise erupted in the worship service. Mary and Alice hugged, and the worship team spontaneously broke into a song of praise. Words could not express the joy at that moment; some broke into applause and others speaking in tongues. Some of us cried tears of joy.

We praise God for what he has done for us, and through us. Sometimes it is important to remember these events in our lives and again lift up our hands and voices in praise. Thanksgiving that overflows into praise comes both from remembering and from hearing a testimony from others. By being attentive to what God has done for us and for our communities, we are deepening our praise to God.

PRAISE FOR WHAT GOD WILL DO

We often don't think about this in our times of praise, but we can praise God for what he is doing now to complete his work of redemption for the nations. God's character is always the same: past, present and future. His work of redemption in the past points to what he is doing around us and what he will complete. Thus, our reading of passages like the following should lead us to praise:

> Then I saw "a new heaven and a new earth," for the first heaven and the first earth had passed away, and there was no longer any sea. I saw the Holy City, the new Jerusalem, coming down out of heaven from God, prepared as a bride beautifully dressed for her husband. And I heard a loud voice from the throne saying, "Look! God's dwelling place is now among the people, and he will dwell with them. They will be his people, and God himself will be with them and be their God. 'He will wipe every tear from their eyes. There will be no more death' or mourning or crying or pain, for the old order of things has passed away." (Rev 21:1-4)

This amazing vision points to what God has been doing, reveals something of who God is, and points to what God will do in the future. When I read this passage I am drawn especially to the final two sentences. God will wipe away every tear; there will be no more suffering and mourning. God is going to do this. God can be trusted because when he told Israel that he would give them a new heart, and that he would send a suffering servant to take away the sins of the world, he did it. Now we read that he will take away suffering and death. Hallelujah!

Many songs of praise look to the future when God's work in Christ Jesus will be fully revealed. These songs of praise are often based upon passages from Revelation but also from other passages of Scripture. The Philippian hymn, as it is often called, shows us how such praise develops from God's work in Jesus in the past, in the present, and how it looks toward the future. It speaks of Christ Jesus

> Who, though he was in the form of God,
>   did not regard equality with God
>   as something to be exploited,
> but emptied himself,
>   taking the form of a slave,
>   being born in human likeness.
> And being found in human form,
>   He humbled himself
>   and became obedient to the point of death—
>   even death on a cross.
>
> Therefore God also highly exalted him
>   and gave him the name
>   that is above every name,
> so that at the name of Jesus
>   every knee should bend,
>   in heaven and on earth and under the earth,
> and every tongue should confess
>   that Jesus Christ is Lord
>   to the glory of God the Father.
>   (Phil 2:5-11 NRSV)

The future, which we can be thankful for in the present, is a time and place where Jesus is honored supremely with no other worship preventing the pure glory of God. Both classic and contemporary Christian praise music poetically and imaginatively lift up visions of God's future glory and our future unmediated relationship with the living God:

I Can Only Imagine
I can only imagine what it will be like
When I walk, by your side.
I can only imagine what my eyes will see

When your face is before me.
I can only imagine.
I can only imagine.
Surrounded by your glory
what will my heart feel?
Will I dance for you Jesus,
or in awe of you be still?
Will I stand in your presence,
or to my knees will I fall?
Will I sing hallelujah?
Will I be able to speak at all?
I can only imagine.
I can only imagine.
I can only imagine when that day comes,
when I find myself standing in the Son.
I can only imagine when all I would do is forever,
forever worship you
I can only imagine.
I can only imagine.[4]

Other praise looks to the future life where God's power and beauty is revealed, but it does so by seeing how this future is anchored to the past. Jesus, the Lamb of God, sacrificed for us, brings about a creation freed from every sin and from all corruption:

Revelation Song
Worthy is the Lamb who was slain
Holy, holy is he.
Sing a new song to him who sits on
Heaven's mercy seat.
Holy, holy, holy is the Lord God Almighty,
Who was and is and is to come.
With all creation I sing praise to the King of kings.
You are my everything and I will adore you.
Clothed in rainbows of living color;
flashes of lightening; rolls of thunder.
Blessing and honor, strength and glory and power be,
to you the only one who is King. . . .

Filled with wonder, awestruck wonder,
At the mention of your name.
Jesus your name is power, breath, and living water;
Such a marvelous mystery.
Oh, You're worthy, mystery
You are worthy.[5]

In some older hymnbooks these types of praise songs are called "hymns of the church triumphant." This means simply that these look to the future, the fulfillment of the church found in heavenly existence. Hymns like "Glorious Things of Thee Are Spoken," and "Lead On, O King Eternal" praise God for the future, assured through the work of Jesus on the cross. Such praise is not an escape from the earthly responsibility of the church; rather, as if we were standing outside of our daily life, we look and see how our labors and prayers point to the future. This future is beautiful, powerful, peaceful, communal; in it all is love because God is fully present, and his glory shines like the sun. It is both an ecstatic and intimate joy.

WORSHIP AND EMOTIONS

Before you continue reading, ask yourself this simple question: What do I think about emotions as a follower of Christ? Are emotions misleading? Are emotions helpful in knowing and experiencing God? Are emotions necessary or unnecessary? Do I think it is better to be rational about the church, worship, and certainly about praise?

When I first came to faith in Jesus Christ I was shown a little booklet (called a tract) that explained what to do with emotions. The outline of the booklet was memorable. There was a little train that had an engine (facts), then it had a passenger car (faith) and then a caboose (feelings). Of the three cars, the caboose was not necessary. It seems to me that the booklet was obviously designed by an engineer or math and science person. I believed the booklet most of my life, with the simple conclusion that feelings can be misleading, so you may let them follow, but don't think they are to lead you anywhere.

I now think this is wrong. The Bible is absolutely filled with feelings, and we are even told to express joy and to even shout with joy. We are designed both to feel things deeply *and* to think clearly about God. God designed us to experience great joy, and this great joy we experience both confirms what we learn and provides a way to know God. In the church, we are invited to come with our whole being to worship (certainly in praise) and to witness. We can be silent and meditative, we listen and are attentive, but we also feel great joy as we praise God.

When we come to church (or more exactly, to worship), we first stand. When we stand to praise, we are standing in the presence of the living God who desires relationship and reshaping of our lives and our world. Our first response to God is always thanksgiving. In fact, the foundation of the Christian life (not just worship) is thanksgiving and praise. We praise God for who he is, what he has done, what he has done for me or us, and what he will do. Praise builds upon memory and thanksgiving, and it involves our whole being. It is a living, joyous participation with the congregation through God's Holy Spirit. This means that praise evokes both power and some mystery.

We may not think about this or feel it in our times of worship on Sunday (or Saturday, or any day of the week), but in fact, praise is more than following instructions. Praise is more than just reciting a history of what God has done. Praise, as it were, is a contact sport.

Praise wells up into our whole being: emotions, body, mind, and will. Praise can be ordered and thoughtful, but it can also become an explosion of joy.

After looking at the reasons for praise, we'll now consider some dimensions and dynamics of praise: emotions, private and corporate praise, cultures and multicultural praise, and we will look at what it means to praise when we don't feel like it. In the end, we will see that the book of Psalms is a wonderful lifelong textbook on praise. First, however, we want to look at how praise involves intimacy and ecstasy.

THE ECSTATIC AND THE INTIMATE

What makes Christian worship possible, as we have noted already, is that God has already acted. God's action *for* us is an action *toward* us. God's incarnation can be described as God stepping out or coming outside of himself (there is no easy imagery for the incarnation and the Trinity) to be in relationship with us. We know that God is never divided or separated, for God is one, and yet we can talk about God's coming as "standing outside" of himself: *ec-static*. His ecstasy (standing outside or away from himself) is to bring greater intimacy. The intimacy that God brings us at times draws us outside of ourselves to be in intimate relationship with God: ecstasy brings intimacy.[6] In the past century, with the rise of Pentecostalism, the charismatic movement, and indigenous churches in Latin America, Africa, and Asia, we are having much more discussion of the meaning of ecstatic experiences. Although this has been a very small part of the tradition of Western churches, we see from the early church (beginning with Acts) that worship, even listening to a good sermon, can overflow to emotionally charged praise. It is a work of the Holy Spirit that is not to be resisted (see Acts 10:44-48).

Let me be clear from the beginning; we do not enter worship or praise to seek or to chase an experience. That would be closer to paganism or some type of addictive behaviors. No, we accept these experiences because they form part of Christian praise. Maybe a historical example will help.

In the past few decades I have been asked many times, as a historian of Asian Christianity, "Why is it that the Korean church grew so rapidly from the very beginning?" Of course I cannot answer that question here, but I can give a few examples of the early experiences of the churches in worship, and this may give us some clues about the growth of Christianity in Korea. I share this because there is a very close relationship between worship and witness or worship and evangelism and church growth.

The earliest Protestant Christianity in Korea grew at a very rapid pace in the north, in and around Pyeongyang. One of the earliest converts was a former Daoist and Confucian who had suffered the loss of his wife, his twins, and his mother all in the same year. When he finally came to faith, he attended worship, and he experienced the Holy Spirit. It was an experience that changed his life. Worship of the living God became part of his healing: it was a thoughtful and emotional spiritual experience. Christian worship is both an *intimate* experience with God—the One who is closer to you than you are yourself—and an *ecstatic* experience with God. Our ecstasy leads to or is interwoven into a deep intimacy with God, and it is based on God's prior ecstasy. Think about this: the incarnation was an ecstatic experience of God that leads to our intimacy with God.

If God had not come to us, there would be no healed relationship, no intimacy.

When Paul was "caught up into the seventh heaven," or when a person worships by speaking in tongues or with dance, it is an ecstatic experience. A little more Korean history may help. In 1893, a recently converted Korean in Pyeongyang, Korea, Kim Chongsop, went to church and for the first time prayed to the God of the ancestors: the God of Abraham, Isaac, and Jacob, *Hananim*.[7] He made the connection that *Hananim* is the name of the Father of Jesus. The fullness of his Korean identity and his life in Christ came together, and he exclaimed:

> I have known and worshipped the greatest and the holiest *Hananim* who is the omnipresent and omnipotent God. Therefore, when I first knelt before God, my heart was filled with humility and my body trembled. I prayed with my true heart and with sincerity. I did not know if my body was in heaven or on earth. I was so filled with inspiration that I felt myself under a big mountain. When I finished the prayer my body was hot and my voice had changed. I experience the transformation of the Holy Spirit. I was filled with joy.[8]

Even though this may seldom be the experience in our times in worship, such experiences are still very consistent with what we have said about praise and what the early church experienced. Praise comes out of our thanksgiving for what we remember about God and what God has done, and what he will do. In Kim Chongsop's ecstatic experience, he made the connection that God (*Hananim*) is the Father of Jesus, he remembered what Jesus had done, and then he was caught up between earth (now) and heaven (the future).

Many great movements of church growth in the world involved similar ecstatic and intimate experiences. The great Shandong Revival in east China in the early twentieth century was marked by remarkable ecstatic experiences that created new intimacies with God and within families and the church. African independent churches[9] also are marked by such experiences of the Holy Spirit, which then become the basis of future praise and (as we will see in chap. 7) witness to the local community.

Worship, especially praise, involves the whole person. It is not just a rational or cerebral expression of thanksgiving as if checking off a list of what we remember to tell God "thank you" for. However, as ecstatic and intimate as our praise may be, it does involve the whole person, and that means it is mindful and thoughtful, not mindless or irrational. Words and Spirit work together in our body to draw us out of our routine and into God's divine and eternal presence.

PRAISE CORPORATE, PRAISE PERSONAL

A certain excitement can charge large groups joyfully praising together or (if at a football game or ice hockey game) cheering after a touchdown or goal. On the other hand, crowds that share anger at an unjust decision or a corrupt official can be both exciting and scary. A particular item of news or seeing the official in person can ignite a crowd, and rioting can follow. Large groups have an energy and excitement that personal time at a remote lodge does not. However, praise is not like a World Series game or an NCAA final. Praise is both corporate and personal, both shared joy and deep solitude.

Ideally, both personal solitude and community praise should flourish in worship. If it is true that praise and thanksgiving are the foundation of worship and the correction of self-sanctification, then praise should pervade our participation in the body of Christ. My wife and I attended a church many years ago that applied this dual concept of praise in the way they structured their weekly gatherings. Their church bulletin looked something like this:

8:15–8:30	Gathering and personal worship
8:30–9:45	Corporate worship
9:45–10:00	Reflection and prayer

We were encouraged to think of worship as starting at 8:15 as a time of personal praise. The beginning of a worship service should be more of a time of personal praise and thanksgiving and less of a time of catching up on the latest news from the high school or from the neighbors. God relates to each person in a worship service, not just to a group or a bunch of random people. Church worship is a corporate activity, but each individual person is, as an individual person, in relationship with the triune God and with others. A personal time of praise can properly place us before God—filled with thanksgiving as we reflect on God's faithfulness during the past week.

We learn from the Psalms as well as from the earliest Christians that corporate worship involves everyone. We have mentioned above that the whole body should be involved in praise as one common voice. At other times the congregation may be involved in praise as a dialogue, a call and response. Psalm 136 provides a good example, showing the corporate nature of praise.

> Give thanks to the LORD, for he is good.
> > *His love endures forever.*
> Give thanks to the God of gods.
> > *His love endures forever.*
> Give thanks to the Lord of lords:
> > *His love endures forever.* (Ps 136:1-3)

Thus, praise is very personal, as we think of what we personally thank God for in our own lives and in the lives of our families. But praise also resounds with an ocean of voices, even trees clapping their hands, in praise of the king of heaven. Since praise involves all of creation and all of the nations, praise is like a kaleidoscope of colors, voices, instruments, and songs.

PRAISE CULTURAL, PRAISE MULTICULTURAL

Praise unites us, and (because of our fallenness) praise can also divide us. How many parents have been raising their children in traditional churches, and by the time the children are in their mid-teens, they begin to pull away? If the parents are specially blessed, their children will find a church or be invited to a church with more young people and more guitars and drums in worship. Many parents, however, lose their children and they never return to church. Much of the divide has to do with culture and worship. In fact, many, if not most of the divisions in churches are less about theology and more about culture and what is culturally appropriate regarding worship, dress, and life. Culture divides and unites.

Anyone who has visited different churches may have had the experience of feeling a little uncomfortable with the music, words, dress, or even the building. I remember visiting a new megachurch in the South. From the outside, the building, which was in fact built as a new church building, looked like a big-box megastore. The parking lot and drive up area looked like a large high school more than a megachurch. No indication from the outside showed that it was a church: no cross, steeple, stained glass (in fact, there was very little glass!). Not even the name gave a hint that it was a church. There was a generic name (which I have conveniently forgotten) like "Coffee and Community" or "Free and Easy" or "Streams of Life." Such a building is a cultural expression of American consumerism. We might ask, Is this an appropriate expression of Christianity in America, or does this miscommunicate something of the gospel of Jesus Christ?

Although we are talking about praise in this chapter, it is a good place to bring up again the concept of *connection* (to Jesus, Scripture, and the early church) and *context* (local culture). If we praise God exactly like the early disciples did, we would speak Aramaic and we would not use instruments (or very few). We would worship only in a Jewish building or in a house. Such worship would have little attraction for others; in fact, very few people in the world would understand it! Contextualization begins with language, but what language and which dialect? Our family worshiped for years in Singapore where churches generally had worship services in two to five languages: Mandarin (plus one or two Chinese dialects), possibly Malay, Tamil, or English. Those who worshiped in Mandarin often spoke Teochew or Hokkien at home. Some of the hymns I quoted above used very formal English (thou, thee), which is foreign to our common speech today. Language is important—very important. But language is only part of culture.

One of the reasons we speak about culture here is because some of the major problems in churches today have to do with praise: "worship wars" is the expression often used. Choosing what instruments to use, what music to sing, whether or not to use any older hymns—the list goes on and on.

If we are coming to worship to listen to our most popular music, we should go home and think it over again. Corporate worship always is based on grace.

In this chapter we have tried to make it clear that praise is our response to what God has done. Praise is built upon remembering. Praise is not our own music therapy.

"I just didn't like the music at that church" is more revealing about the life of the worshiper than about the church. Perfect worship will come, but in this life we need to extend grace and learn to appreciate cultural expressions (including those of music) that differ from our own taste.

Praise should always come out of the life and community of the local church. However, in our modern and very connected world, praise should also lead us into other cultures. We should expect our worship to be praise lifted up to God and also reaching out to other cultures. We will not sing with the full choir of all the languages of the world until heaven, but in this world, we can and should begin to see our praise as more than monocultural.

We worshiped for a number of years in a church in the East End of Pittsburgh. The local community was 60 percent African American, 30 percent white, and 10 percent from other cultures. Worship services were culturally very mixed, including Asians, Egyptians, and there was also a congregation embedded in our building made up of French-speaking West Africans. The church had a choir, a beautiful organ, grand piano, and hymnals. But the church also had an electric keyboard, guitars, and percussion instruments. Much of the music was black Gospel and contemporary praise music. Sometimes we sang West African choruses. It was not only appropriate, but necessary to sing praises with many different rhythms, melodies, and even languages. Most of the congregation loved the great variety of praise. Some protested, however, with little joy on their faces (if their faces even appeared before the praise was

> Praise is not our own music therapy.

over). Every church needs their community discourse to consider what is culturally appropriate in order to include more and exclude fewer in worship.

GIVE ME A PSALM

When I was in seminary I was often given the opportunity to lead in worship at a local church. Still befuddled by traditional language of mainline churches (Is *offertory* when they take up the money, or is it the music that is played or sung when they take the money?), I was asked to give a prayer of invocation and call to worship. I looked at old bulletins to see what *invocation* meant. I knew it meant "to call on" from the Latin I learned in high school (*voco, vocare, vocati, vocatus*), but I hadn't really heard many prayers of invocation that called on God to be present. That seemed like bad theology. Isn't God already here? So, I did what most pastors and worship leaders do (so I have learned). They go to the Psalms. The Psalms show us how to pray and especially how to praise in the midst of storms, victories, and when reflecting on our past.

The early church had an understanding that each and every psalm is christological. That means that you can find Jesus Christ in each and every psalm.

It is true. The Psalms point to Jesus, and they point to how we can see God and speak to God. For a period of about five years I only preached about Jesus from the Psalms. It wasn't really that difficult, and it reinforced for me that much of the praise in the Psalms does point to Jesus. Psalm 23 is an easy one: Jesus is the Good Shepherd who protects, comforts, and provides for us. But even the longest Psalm, 119, we can see as speaking not only about God's law (statutes, word, etc.), but about God's Word, Jesus Christ.

More significantly, the Psalms guide us in how to praise God. A few examples will be enough to start you on your own study of the Psalms for praise. Psalm 150, the last psalm, tells us *where* we can praise God, *why* we praise God, *how* we are to praise God, and *who* is to praise God. *Where* do we praise God? "Praise the Lord. Praise God in his sanctuary; praise him in his mighty heavens." Today we might say this means we should praise God in the church building as the angels praise God in the heavenlies.

Why do we praise God? "Praise him for his acts of power; praise him for his surpassing greatness." As discussed earlier in this chapter, we are called to praise God for what he has done (his mighty deeds) and for who he is (surpassing greatness).

How are we to praise God? "Praise him with the sounding of the trumpet, praise him with the harp and lyre, praise him with timbrel and dancing, praise him with strings and pipe, praise him with the clash of cymbals, praise him with resounding cymbals." Thus, we are to imaginatively praise God with all the instruments we have. And we are also to praise God with some volume: "loud clashing cymbals!" is more than a soft song of love. There are times of soft singing, but praise of the Lord of the universe is no secret, and it is not to be unobtrusive.

Finally, from this remarkable psalm we learn *who* is to praise God. "Let everything that has breath praise the Lord. Praise the Lord." Well, that says it all. If you are breathing, you have fulfilled the only qualification needed to praise the Lord.

Of course we learn about prayer in every psalm, but in addition almost every psalm teaches us specifically about praise. A few more examples may help. In Psalm 66 we see again both that praise flows from what God has done ("How awesome are your deeds!") and that personal testimony is part of praise ("Come and hear. . . . I will tell you what he has done *for me*."). In Psalm 68 we are reminded that it is appropriate to enter into worship with praise (Ps 68:24-27) and that all of the nations are invited to praise (Ps 68:31-32). In fact, any new church, or any church looking afresh at their worship would do well to spend a year in Psalms. The present author recommends reading a psalm a day, along with reading other Scripture. Really. Every day.

WHEN WE DON'T FEEL LIKE PRAISE

As I write this chapter on praise, my daily routine is entwined with prayers for a close friend whose cancer has returned after eight years of being cancer free. Cancer is neither polite nor predictable. This recent diagnosis means a complete redirecting of the next six to nine months of my friend's life, and it means a sudden disruption in community living of another fifteen or twenty close friends. We are on call to help, support, and pray, and almost every day we will be conscious of the shadow of death passing between us. At this point it is only a shadow. How do I go to worship and praise God now?

There have been times like this when I have not felt like praising God at all. There are many different reasons for this. Life just does not seem to be going well, people seem to be against us, and (as we all know) sometimes we just want to stay in bed and sleep. We get depressed, feel persecuted, or just don't want to be with other people. And we get angry. In fact, sometimes we get angry at people we will have to see at worship. One of the great ironies is that we usually need to remember what God has done and give him praise at the very times we are the most depressed or angry. Who wants to go to a worship service and sit next to a family who has gossiped about your daughter? No one really. But at times like that, what better place is there to be than in the presence of a holy, truthful, gracious, and forgiving God?

I wish we didn't have conflicts with people in the church, but we do. Forgiveness is one of the most difficult things we will ever have to do in life. Praising God in hard times may be the second hardest thing to do.

We must affirm that the conditions for praise do not rest on us, but on God. We do not praise God *because* we are happy or feeling thankful. We praise God on the very *eternal* reality that God is love and has loved us more than we can imagine or than we can fully appreciate. Thanksgiving, leading to praise, provides a deep foundation for our lives. On that foundation we build our own Christian growth, and part of that growth involves suffering and lament. Lament, which comes from the Latin word for weeping, is an appropriate response to suffering and pain. There are times in life when the only prayer we feel we can utter is a prayer of lament to God. We cry out to God and tell him of our pain, our loss, our loneliness.

But this lament (or even our confession of sin) does not change who God is, what God has done, and who I am in relationship to God.

At a point of terrible grief and loss in my own life, I just wanted to go away. I would go to the office and sit by my window with the blinds almost completely closed and the lights off. Hours would pass and I could only stare off into the cracks of sunlight through the blinds. I was teaching in a seminary and would avoid lunch and chapel. I seemed to be thinking to myself, "If praise is a response to who God is and what God has done, then how in the world can I praise God now in the shadow of two deaths?" Two close family members died suddenly in an accident; I was lost. But there were times in those months of depression that the Spirit of the living God would remind me that God is still God. With great effort I would get up, walk to the door, turn the handle, open the door and slowly and deliberately walk down the hall to chapel. I would sit in the back of the chapel, trying to avoid talking to anyone. As much as anything it was the songs of praise that reminded me of who I am and who God is. God became my shelter and my shepherd again. It was a slow process, but I slowly rebuilt my life of worship and praise. That rebuilding required willful commitment to the community and to praise—praise that did not seem inviting at all at the time.

It is dishonest to pretend everything is OK when it is not, but it is also dishonest to think God is not worthy of praise when life is difficult. Life is difficult much of the time. Praise is still in season, all of the time.

POWER AND PRAISE

In our daily lives we may have a hard time equating praise with power, but this is actually the case. In the above personal case, praise had the power to heal and bring me out of depression or to bring me into a new and more hopeful life. As Christians, we know about (and experience every day) the brokenness of creation and the evil that pervades our world. At times we feel powerless to make a difference or even to resist the strong pull toward self-worship. That is what our struggle really is about: worshiping or honoring ourselves above all else. This is the original sin of Adam and Eve in the garden, and it is the basic sinful tendency of all humans after them. The power that propels us to be selfish when we know we should be giving, that entraps us in frivolous and vain entertainment when we know we should grow in love of others, and finally, the lack of control that we seem to have over our own thought life. All of these experiences cloud our understanding of praise. But this is sin on a personal level.

On a more pervasive or even cosmic level, all of creation is fallen and in need of redemption. Praise has a cosmic, not just a personal and communal, dimension. We read in Romans:

> For the creation waits in eager expectation for the children of God to be revealed. For the creation was subjected to frustration, not by its own choice, but by the will of the one who subjected it, in hope that the creation itself will be liberated from its bondage to decay and brought into the freedom of the glory of the children of God.
>
> We know that the whole creation has been groaning as in the pains of childbirth right up to the present time. Not only so, but we ourselves, who have the firstfruits of the Spirit, groan inwardly as we wait for our adoption to sonship, the redemption of our bodies. (Rom 8:19-23)

We are part of that fallen creation that groans until all is redeemed. Creation, all of God's creation, is redeemed through Jesus Christ. The full expression of this redemption comes about in part through the praise of God's people. Remember, praise expresses the truth about God, creation, and who we are as God's much-loved creatures. God inhabits the praises of his people (Ps 22:3 KJV). In praise, God actually takes up residence. God enters into our places and times of praise. Praise is more than singing a song, doing a call and response Psalm, or a time of shouts of praise and speaking in tongues. Praise brings us into the presence of the all-powerful God who wants all of life to be redeemed. As we read above in Romans 8, all of creation longs for this freedom of the glory of the children of God. Praise is an essential element of that process.

We find another important passage that connects power to praise in Acts. It is the story of Paul and Silas when being persecuted for their faith, a time of genuine powerlessness.

> After they had been severely flogged, they were thrown into prison, and the jailer was commanded to guard them carefully. When he received these orders, he put them in the inner cell and fastened their feet in the stocks.

> About midnight Paul and Silas were praying and singing hymns to God, and the other prisoners were listening to them. Suddenly there was such a violent earthquake that the foundations of the prison were shaken. At once all the prison doors flew open, and everyone's chains came loose. (Acts 16:23-26)

Now we should not assume from this one passage that praise always does such remarkable things. Nevertheless, many stories from missionaries and church leaders in regions where the gospel is being proclaimed for the first time tell about such power observed. Praise has the power to convert, to convict, and to continue the work of transformation in an individual or a community.

Many great revivals have begun—in China, Korea, Northeast India, New England, Indonesia, California, England, East Africa—from times of praise. We should expect praise to have power.

Finally, it should be noted that the whole book of Revelation, a book often misunderstood because of the symbolism, is really a book about praise and worship. The Revelation came to John "on the Lord's day." In other words, on the day of worship, John was "in the Spirit" and the vision came to him (Rev 1:10). He recorded the vision, a vision filled with symbols, images of creatures, and some battles. What is often missed in interpreting Revelation is the power of worship, specifically praise. Throughout the book Jesus is depicted as ruling, either as the Lamb, or as a man in white with a sword for a tongue. Jesus reigns, and the nations, along with the heavenly creatures and angels, all worship. Victory over all evil comes not from direct battles, but from praise. When God is praised, evil is vanquished. Praise permeates the revelation! We have glimpses of heavenly worship in chapter 4, but also in chapter 5, chapter 7, chapter 11, chapters 12, 14, and 19, and then in the last three chapters (Rev 20–22). Revelation ends with one of the reasons we praise God. We praise God for what he will do.

> I did not see a temple in the city, because the Lord God Almighty and the Lamb are its temple. The city does not need the sun or the moon to shine on it, for the glory of God gives it light, and the Lamb is its lamp. The nations will

walk by its light, and the kings of the earth will bring their splendor into it. On no day will its gates ever be shut, for there will be no night there. The glory and honor of the nations will be brought into it. (Rev 21:22-26)

There is power in praise: power over Satan, power over sin, and power to redeem.

Let everything that has breath praise the LORD. (Ps 150:6)

5

KNEEL

SOME TIME BACK I WAS INVITED to preach at a Christian college for their chapel service. Arriving a little early to get the microphone adjusted and to go over the "order of worship,"[1] I met a young man whom, it appeared, had cerebral palsy and needed a walker to steady himself when walking. I introduced myself to him and he responded, "Yes, I know who you are! Welcome." Before the service he walked around the worship space mumbling to himself or to God. Then, when the service was about to begin, the young man slowly came down the side aisle and came up next to me (in the front row) and sat down. I leaned over and asked him to pray for me. "I have been; that is why I come early," he responded. The praise music, prayers, and Scripture reading—which were beautifully done—began, and we all rose to our feet. Soon my new friend raised his hands firmly with wrists slightly bent pointing out. Singing with great vigor he thrust his hands skyward, and looked up to heaven. By the second song his praise turned from standing with hands raised to kneeling down in gestures of contrition and humility. He was kneeling on the floor. By the third song he pushed away the walker, spread out his hands and lay face down on the floor as in the very presence of the Living Christ. I could almost hear, "Go away from me, Lord; I am a sinful man!" (Lk 5:8). His worship moved from standing in prayer to kneeling (even prostrate) in confession.

In the presence of a great athlete, we all look pretty feeble. In the presence of a great opera singer, we all sound pretty flat. When in the presence of a holy God, we all are exposed as sinners. In worship we begin with praise, focusing on who God is and what God has done and what

God will do. After we focus for a while on God, we then look around us and remember who we are. We are a fallen people, whose image of God has been dirtied and clouded by our sin and by society's net that entraps us in sinful behaviors, attitudes, and thought patterns. We do not deserve to be in the presence of such a wonderful, beautiful, pure, and loving God. We recognize anew that we are sinners. Thus, the third body movement is to kneel. Come to Jesus. Stand to praise. Kneel to confess our sins.

SIN . . . OR MISTAKES?

Sin is not a common word today. In fact, a chart of word frequency would show that the word *sin* has declined in the frequency of usage in the twentieth century and into the first decades of the twenty-first century. We do not like to talk about, think about, or even consider the concept of sin. Modern Western societies live in denial, as if sin does not exist, or as if it only exists in the most hardened of criminals. Most of us know we are not perfect, but we prefer to think of it as mistakes we make, or ways that other people *cause* us to sin. "It was not really my fault. I can't help it if her paper was close enough for me to see the answers. I pretty much knew the right answer even before I looked at her paper." I am not really responsible for my imperfections and compromises.

Let's bring back sin! Or at least let's bring back the use of the word; as long as we don't talk about sin, its power remains. Being unwilling to talk about cancer will kill you. Sin is a cancer. Its power lies in our denial and inattention to its presence. As long as we do not admit to sin, the ongoing memory and the resultant guilt remain. Sin does not end in the actual thought or act; it becomes a disease planted in our soul that will not die. It remains, and we become less than we were meant to be as long as that disease remains.

Let me put this in perspective. Parents are always hoping that their children will confess to something they have done, but none of us want to actually confess what we have done (or thought). When older brother finds the scissors and tries them out on younger brother's hair or when a teenage child comes home late and smells of alcohol, parents want a confession more than perfection.

We don't expect our children to be perfect, but we would like them to be honest, and we want them to trust us to forgive them. We are looking for an honest, "Father, I have offended you." Or at least, "sorry, Mom" would be such a wonderful thing to hear. This is music to a parent's ears. A new intimacy and level of trust can all come out of an honest confession. And yet it is so, so hard to confess. Let's look at this more closely.

General confession is much easier. It is not so hard to say, "I know I am imperfect and I do some things that are bad, that displease God." Or a child, to avoid facing their guilt might say, "Gosh, Mom, of course I'm not perfect! What do you expect?" This says, "Back off, I don't want to deal with what I have done. Let's change the subject. Please!" Most of us at some point have done this and then we want to move on with our life. We don't want to face our specific offenses directly, just generically. But Christian confession is not to be so generic and flippant. Confession that a parent wants to hear is a little more self-effacing and humble. "Dad, I am sorry. I know you trusted me with the car, but I took it out on a back road where you told me not to go, and I think I ruined the front right suspension. I am sorry, Dad; I hope you can forgive me." That is what a parent wants to hear, and when we hear it, we generally are so very thankful and are then willing to work at rebuilding trust with our child. There are consequences to such behavior, but the open confession of a child connected to a parental embrace prevents an irreparable consequence: a broken relationship. God is called Father, and he is even a much better parent than what I have described above.

When Nancy and I visited all those churches (the visits that led to the idea for this book), the most important element of the church that was missing was confession. Not only in the worship service itself, but in the literature, bulletins, libraries, and conversation, we saw little to no evidence of a life of confession. In light of our earlier discussion of *connection* and *context*, we can say that this important connection with the life of Jesus (who even submitted to baptism) and the early church was missing. Very few churches we attended had anything close to a confession of sin. Many (most?) worship services moved from praise (usually only through music) to offering, or they moved from praise to sermon with no pause to reflect on our own sinfulness in the presence of a holy God. Calls to confess and repent fill Scripture, both as prescriptions (what we are to do) and historic descriptions (what has happened).

> While I kept silent,
>   my bones wasted away
>   through my groaning all day long.
> For day and night
>   your hand was heavy on me;
> my strength was sapped
>   as in the heat of summer.
> Then I acknowledged my sin to you
>   and did not cover up my iniquity.
> I said, "I will confess
>   my transgressions to the LORD."
> And you forgave
>   the guilt of my sin. (Ps 32:3-5)

Experiences of confession and repentance occur when people come into God's presence. Here are two classic examples:

> "Woe to me!" I cried. "I am ruined! For I am a man of unclean lips, and I live among a people of unclean lips, and my eyes have seen the King, the LORD Almighty." (Is 6:5)

> But when Simon Peter saw this [the huge catch of fish], he fell at Jesus' knees and said, "Go away from me, Lord; I am a sinful man!" (Lk 5:8)

Praise at its best brings us into God's presence, and when we come into God's presence, we remember who God is and how broken we are.

We can also look at this dynamic from a different angle. When we come into worship and praise God we are caught up between heaven and earth, between what is now and what is to be. Worship reorients us. We realize again *who* we are by seeing *whose* we are. But in the presence of such holiness and beauty we then recognize our finiteness and our imperfection. As with Isaiah in the presence of the holy God in Isaiah 6, or Peter, who recognized who Jesus was in the miraculous catch of fish on the shores of Lake Gennesaret, our response is one of humility and even fear.

In praise we are invited into God's presence, but his presence is awesome, or awe-inspiring, or awe-full. As we praise God we come to realize who God is:

- powerful

- creative

- pure

- beautiful

- perfect

- surprising

- gentle

- merciful

- knowledgeable

- kind

- loving

Coming into God's presence exposes us. We cannot hide from God when we worship him, so what do we do? The proper and even natural response should be to say something as simple as, "Help me!" This cry admits sin, guilt, and inability. But what really is confession and how does it relate to repentance?

WHAT IS NOT CONFESSION

A few years back Nancy and I were in a worship service and, after about twenty-five minutes of beautiful praise music (a little Gospel with rock and some hymn-like melodies), it was time for confession. The church we were visiting was a regular, old-fashioned, big, inner-city Presbyterian church that was now reaching out more to the local community of African Americans, African immigrants, and university students. A very diverse gathering each Sunday, including a number of biracial couples who had found a home where they were received and their ministries and children accepted without question.

This particular day, however, the prayer of confession was a little strange. Whether because of the pastor's own life, or a difficult week of counseling church members, we were invited to enter into a corporate confession that went something like this:

> Lord, we come to you as your children and yet this week we have offended you in many ways. We are deeply sorry. We confess that we have given in to pride, and we have been angry without cause. We have also been unfaithful to our spouses, committing adultery, and we have been violent to our children. . . .

At this point I tuned out, slowly opened my eyes, and checked to see if other people were also feeling a little uncomfortable. I was sitting next to my lovely wife, whom I had not been angry at; I had not in any way considered adultery. I was thinking about our children, whom we had not beaten, that week or any week! Now I am sure I had proud thoughts, admittedly. And, as with all of us, I had offended God in many ways, some known to me and other ways not even known.

This brings up an important point about confession. When it is done publically, it is healthy to use some of the great prayers of confession that have been used for centuries (see examples below). Human nature and "falling short of the glory of God" has not changed that much, really. When we try to wing it and write something relevant and honest, we may get carried away. I quietly mentioned to the pastor on my way out that her prayer of confession was a little too specific and graphic for me. It also misrepresented most of us (at least I hope so!). So, public confession is not listing specific sins that only some may have committed.

What else is not confession? A generic "I'm sorry" to God is not confession. Such an expression may be the beginning of confession, but confession is not just a matter of expressing a feeling; it also deals with facts, historic facts. Again, an analogy using children may be helpful. Let's say that child A opened his brother's drawer where he keeps his candy and, while brother B was in school, took two of B's favorite candy bars and ate them. B returns from school and discovers the theft. When confronted at dinner about the candy bar theft, A says "I'm sorry." He may even (if he is very young) simply say, "I'm sorry that your candy was taken." B gets a little angry, "But did you take it?" "If your candy is gone, I'm sorry that it is gone." True confession is more like George Washington and the cherry tree (as the story has been told for a couple of centuries). "Yes, father, I cut down the cherry tree." In the candy caper, brother A, with no excuses or explanation simply says, "Brother B, yes, I went in your room, opened your candy drawer, and stole some of your candy. I am sorry. I will get you more candy tomorrow."

Confession is not a general "I'm sorry" whispered to the walls. Nor is it a nonspecific guilt that we try to cover over with general, non-specific statements of apology. Confession is also not disconnected from repentance. To confess is to admit that you did something wrong: "I am sorry that I gossiped about you to the class." But confession without the intent to change behavior is not confession either. If you confess gossip and then next week gossip again and again and get your little thrill from putting someone down, well, you have not made a genuine confession. Confession says, "I am sorry and I realize that this behavior is wrong. God, help me to step away from (gossip, stealing, yelling, pride, etc.)." Confession launches us to repentance.

CONFESSION IS A COMMUNAL ACT

Protestants are good with words—preaching, teaching and reading Scripture—but not as good with body movement (well, except for Pentecostals). I based this book on the image of the embodied church and symbolized its practices as body movements. However, for this chapter I would like to call upon the image of a large cathedral when the time for the prayer of confession is announced. The whole congregation reaches down to pull out the kneelers and all drop to their knees in an attitude of contrition. Businessmen, teachers, mothers, children, police officers, and the homeless all drop to their knees in humility. The image includes the sound of bodies sliding off of pews, kneelers hitting the ground and clothes rustling as hundreds of people in a symphony of humility lower themselves before a holy God. Confession is something we all do as one family of faith. We have our individual sins, but we also sin corporately.

It is good and healthy to confess as a community of believers. Well-thought-out prayers remind us of biblical images of confession and of the great tradition of confession over the centuries. Sin is not a new thing at all. And our sinning is not really that original. We sin by commission (I did something wrong) and omission (I neglected to do something good). Our sins still circle around pride, anger, and impure thoughts. So we confess these sins as a body.

But in addition, as a body we have blind spots. We are greedy or avaricious as a culture. As a culture we tend to be materialistic, not trusting God as we should. As a culture we tend to be racist and self-serving. Confession of sins as a body reminds us, the church, that we need (together) to fight against the dark side of our culture and our community and our nation. Confession hamstrings the power our culture has over us.

> Confession hamstrings the power our culture has over us.

Although in the West we think we have to invent something new every time we launch a new initiative, that is not true. In the ancient world—and even up to the eighteenth century—people assumed that what was old was true. *New* generally meant wrong, getting off the track of truth. Today we have the opposite impulse: what is new is true. I would like to suggest that many new things (including novels, stories, and music) are not better than classic presentations. The same is true of prayers. True prayer does not have to be new or made up on the spot. Great prayers in the past were prayed over and written down carefully. God has truly inspired many great prayers, most of which are filled with Scripture. Not all old prayers are great, but some are. It is helpful at times to settle ourselves down, take off the pressure of praying something new and true (this can be a lot of pressure!) and pray a trusted ancient prayer that has brought our sisters and brothers through the ages to their knees.

Some prayers of confession. Take a few moments to read over these prayers of confession. No: don't just read over them; meditate over these prayers. Pray them.

Most merciful God, we confess that we have sinned against you in thought, word, and deed, by what we have done, and by what we have left undone. We have not loved you with our whole heart; we have not loved our neighbors as ourselves. We are truly sorry and we humbly repent, for the sake of your Son Jesus Christ, have mercy on us and forgive us; that we may delight in your will, and walk in your ways, to the glory of your Name. Amen. (*Book of Common Prayer*)

Eternal God, in whom we live and move and have our being, whose face is hidden from us by our sins, and whose mercy we forget in the blindness of our hearts: cleanse us from all our offenses, and deliver us from proud thoughts and vain desires, that with reverent and humble hearts we may draw near to you, confessing our faults, confiding in your grace, and finding in you our refuge and strength; through Jesus Christ your Son. (*Book of Common Worship*, PCUSA, 1993)

Almighty and most merciful Father,
We have wandered and strayed from your ways like lost sheep.
We have followed too much the devices and desires of our own hearts.
We have offended against your holy laws.
We have left undone those things that we ought to have done;
And we have done those things that we ought not to have done.
And there is no health in us.
But you Lord, have mercy on us sinners.
Spare those who confess their faults.
Restore those who are penitent,
According to your promises declared to mankind, in Christ Jesus our Lord.
And grant, O most merciful Father, for His sake,
That we may live a disciplined, righteous and godly life,
To the glory of your holy name.
Amen. ("Morning Prayer," *Book of Common Prayer*, 1928)

Communal confession is important because groups of people do get caught up into sinful patterns of thought and behavior. Churches become racist. Churches can become classist. Churches can become self-serving and proud. When this happens, a whole church needs to confess how it has ignored the neighborhood and the local needs, caring only about its members. Other groups, such as families, nations, and races, sin and need to confess the sins of the past so they can move forward. As long as the nationalistic or racist sins of the past remain unconfessed, not brought to public light, the sin remains as a disease. As we all know it is far too easy to return to older patterns of behavior when sin has not been confessed.

CONFESSION IS VERY PERSONAL

Confession is also so very personal that we do not want anyone at all to know what we have thought, what we have seen, what we have said, what we have done, or what we have dreamed. Not only is it embarrassing, what has gone on in our mind would also break many relationships if others knew what we had thought about. However, it is only when we plumb the depths of our own memory to uncover the buried garbage of pride, greed, and lust that we can really be healed. As long as we cover over the sinful memories, the guilt remains, and as long as the guilt remains, it eats away at us. Like hazardous materials buried in leaky containers, our unconfessed sins seep into the soil of our souls.

> Like hazardous materials buried in leaky containers, our unconfessed sins seep into the soil of our souls.

Let me put this in perspective by looking to Jesus. Why did Jesus come to earth? Did Jesus just come to see what it was really like to be a human? "Wow, this is really interesting. I had no idea it was so dirty here! This food really tastes good, though."

That is ridiculous. Jesus didn't come to earth just to get the inside story on his creation. Jesus did not come for many reasons, even though the results of his coming include quite a variety. Jesus came to earth for one reason only. He came to redeem creation through conquering sin and its power to kill.

Jesus came to deal with sin.

Now there are many ways one might deal with sin. The way we deal with sinful behavior in our civic life is to arrest and punish. You have to pay for your sins. Are you involved in drug trafficking? You will pay for it in prison. Did you steal your neighbor's car or lawn mower? You will pay for it. We reason that if the sin is large enough, the punishment must also be sufficiently large. The most ancient law regarding sin is a very simple one that points toward justice. It is easy to remember, and it is a basic principle for dealing with sin: "An eye for an eye and a tooth for a tooth" (Ex 21:24).

We see this way of dealing with sin in much of the Old Testament. God warns Israel (through the prophets and often to the kings) to follow God. If you do follow God's law, you will be blessed. If not, you will be punished, and punishment will eventually mean you will lose your nation and be sent into exile. You will lose everything. However, God does not completely reject Israel if they sin, because underlying God's judgment on sin is God's grace. God still loves his people. The law has its consequences, but love remains.

In both of these cases—breaking the law and Israel's rejecting God's law—punishment follows. Our sin brings punishment also. However, as we know, the miracle of life in Jesus Christ is that Jesus himself takes the punishment we deserve, and so we receive mercy.

Confession releases mercy and grace. This is the most amazing way of dealing with sin: someone else pays the price. Confession is the doorway to grace. Thus, personal confession extends the joyful opportunity for us to turn our sin over to Jesus and have him take care of it for us. For our own health and wholeness, we need to *remember*, *recite*, and then *release*. We remember our sins as specific acts and thoughts we have had. Sometimes this is very painful because we can't believe we have thought such terrible things about others. When we remember them, we need to recite them. We do not need to shout them, but maybe whisper them to Jesus, who is waiting for us to admit what has separated us from him. Remember, recite, and then release.

When we release these thoughts and actions to Jesus we are also repenting of such behaviors for the future. We are saying in essence, "Here you go Jesus. I am so sorry. Please take this mess of mine and give me your spirit to think and do what is pleasing to you."

Advice on vice: A little detour. I would like to take a little detour here. I think that much of the impotency of our churches comes not from our being a bunch of forgiven sinners, but from being unforgiven sinners—going around hiding our sins and putting on a good Christian smile much of the time. Technology and our highly privatized Western life nurture our spiritual impotence. We can hide our pride and self-centeredness through being active on social media. Much of our social media presence is self-promotion made easy and acceptable. Unpopular as this view may be, I believe the internet encourages both lust and greed. Commerce fuels the internet, and one of the greatest producers is pornography. Self-absorption is endemic to our society today, and it is important that we personally admit how our thoughts are more shaped by the media culture. We also need to confess this corporately. This would be a good discussion for your church: How do our phones, computers, and other technology feed basic sins of lust, greed, and pride?

If you get to a point where you are stuck in confession it helps to remember what the early church knew so well. The basic vices or sins that entrap us are three in number. They are translated in various ways, but as a memory aid, we can remember "Pretty Sinful Guy/Gal": PSG. PSG stands for Pride, Sensual Pleasure, and Greed. The stool of sin rests on these three legs. Our pride, our search for sensual pleasure, and our greed for more possessions or more money lead us astray. Murder mystery writers know this so well. Almost every murder is solved by identifying the clear motive and opportunity. Often the detectives question a suspect in search for the motive. If someone appears to have committed the murder and there is no clear motive, the police are baffled. "She had no motive. Why would she have poisoned her neighbor?" In fact, in a very enlightening episode of the British crime series *Inspector Morse*, Morse summarizes for his junior partner the cause of all crimes. To paraphrase, "In my experience all crimes have as their root cause the love of money, personal power, or sex. That is all." Well, that is a British inspector on a BBC television series, not Scripture, but he is pretty close.

We do not need to dwell on these here, but it is helpful to remember when we are confessing our sin, we often find that we were led to sin by our own pride (seeking the attention of others), our sensual pleasure (which can be for food as well as for sexual experience), or wanting nicer clothes, more money, or the newest phone/game/car: pride, sensual pleasure, and greed.

CONFESSION IS AN ICON OF HUMILITY

An icon is an image that points to a greater truth or a deeper view of what is divine and holy. Holy icons are representations of saints that symbolize all that the saint's life means for us as we meditate on the image. Icons are windows or doors into the life and virtues of the saint. We now have a very common use for this sacred word *icon* today. We now use the same language of icons for little pictures on our computers or phones. Icons on our computers are little pictures or symbols that open up the door to everything represented by the image. Click on the icon and you enter a whole new world. Confession is a type of icon. Confession of our sins before a holy God is an image—especially if we kneel to confess—of our humility before God. For this reason we use the body movement of kneeling for confession. This posture brings to mind the humility of the captured enemy or of the servant who kneels before royalty. Confession is a symbol of humility. Why is this important?

There are many ways of looking at or describing the Christian life. One way to do this asks, What are the most important characteristics of the Christian? We can easily argue that love is the most important character trait of the Christian. Or we could argue for grace or mercy: the Christian forgives others. However, for the early church, the supreme virtue of the Christian was humility. They saw the humility of Jesus, his willingness to submit to vain, weak, and unjust human authority as the supreme example of humility. Jesus, who was actually God on earth, humbled himself and submitted to human authority, even to the point of death (Phil 2:6-8). We are invited to live such a life that, in its humility and even humiliation, brings resurrection and power.

Humility's power comes from its truth.

Humility's power comes from its truth. When we humble ourselves before God, admitting our guilt, we are expressing truth. I really *do* need help. I really *cannot* do it on my own. Nancy and I attended a church once where the pastor had a constant refrain that was so helpful to hear. After reading a passage, or in the middle of a sermon, he would summarize a point by saying, "I can't, but he can." The meaning was simple. It was a small confession of humility. Only God is able to save me, to give me wisdom, to guide me, to enable me to do good for others, and on and on. Humility is truth speaking.

The two most-prayed prayers in the world also recognize this simple truth about humility and confession. The Lord's Prayer starts out in praise and then turns to confession (much like this book): "Our Father in heaven, hallowed be your name, your kingdom come, your will be done, on earth as it is in heaven. Give us today our daily bread. And forgive us our sins, as we also have forgiven those who have sinned against us.[2] And lead us not into temptation" (Mt 6:9-13). We submit a humble request for bread in the midst of prayer and confession.

The second prayer, probably prayed even more because it is so brief, is the Jesus Prayer. This ancient prayer continues to be prayed mostly among Eastern Christians (Orthodox as well as Roman Catholic) and increasingly among Protestants in the West. It is a simple prayer that places us correctly before God: "Lord Jesus Christ, Son of God, have mercy on me, a sinner." Seeking God's mercy is a position of extreme humility. It is a recognition, like my Bible church pastor of many years ago, that "I can't, but he can."

Confession is an icon of humility. Humility is our true, healthy, and empowered self.

CONFESSION, REST, AND SILENCE

Although we are talking mostly about church by using corporate worship as the framework, it needs to be mentioned that confession takes time, lots of time—more time than allowed in a weekly worship service. Most of us are so busy with life's concerns and responsibility that we barely have time to pay our monthly bills, forget considering what sins require confession (well, actually, all sins require confession). We need time. We need time to reflect on who we are, what we have done this past week, when and where we got caught up in behaviors that were displeasing to God. I think most of us, if given a minute to confess their sins, would draw a blank.

For this reason, it is a good and healthy practice to have longer periods of time to reflect on our relationship to a holy God and to ask God to gently shine the light of the gospel into the dark places of our lives. It is far too easy for us to cover over our sinfulness, our self-centeredness, and to go through life more self-absorbed than we realize. We need silence because our days are filled with noise and images that bombard us with messages that seldom point toward confession and humility. Most of the messages we receive entice us to be something we are not meant to be: a consumer or a devotee of goods and services. Without stepping away from the constant messages, images, and noise, our discipleship becomes less about Jesus and more about cultural conditioning.

Therefore, silence must be connected to a different type of conditioning: the shaping that comes from Scripture (the topic of the next chapter). If we finally sit down to be silent and think about God and ask for his Spirit to guide us to confession, all we may think about may be the world around us. For this reason, it is important to read, meditate upon, and even memorize Scripture. Then when we turn off all our technology, sit still, and remain silent, we find an opening for God's Word to actually speak to us. Being filled with Scripture helps us in our confession. The beauty, holiness, and gentleness of God will rise up in us and convict us of our own sin. This is very good and necessary for us to grow as Christians. Silence, in the presence of a holy God, will lead to conviction and eventually to confession and repentance.

Confession and repentance are the two hands of the life of humility. In confession we stand before a holy and loving God and admit what we have done and what we have thought. Where do these terrible thoughts come from? In repentance we seek to change our behavior. In fact, the two are (or should be) integrally related. It does little good to admit to a sin you intend to commit again and again. That is not genuine confession.

In fact, it is a lie. True confession leads to remorse and a search to change behaviors and patterns of thinking. More than anything else, the humility of confession—which requires us to live in truth—is the major step in changing our behaviors and thoughts. Admitting we need help (whether it be the alcoholic or the proud teacher or the gossip) is a major step toward change.

Confession and daily repentance could have saved many a failed pastorate and many a failed businessperson or politician. When we think more highly of ourselves than we should, we open the door to moral failure and misrepresenting God. We begin to believe the lie that we are living. When we hear about the moral failure of a Christian leader, we should immediately ask ourselves, what is preventing me from such a failure? Pride or self-confidence will lead you to such moral failure. We begin to think we are above the law or able to live in the midst of unnecessary temptations without getting stained. Confession will save us from moral failure, because it brings us back again and again to Jesus, who sees through us, forgives us, and receives us back.

"Thank you, Jesus, for revealing my sin and embracing me."

CONFESSION IN A WORLD OF LITTLE SIN

Since I had previously lived and taught in Singapore, I was often called upon when Asian guests or students came to our seminary when I was teaching in the United States. One day a new student from China came in my office. Assuming he was a Christian (why else would he study at an American seminary?), I found out that he was actually a university graduate working on a master's degree in Beijing. Even though a Communist party member, he wanted to study Christian theology for a year. I told him the best way to study Christian theology was to attend church. I introduced him to a good (very evangelistic) Chinese language church in the city. After a few months of attending he came into my office.

"What I don't understand about Christianity is that you believe that Jesus died for your sins. But what if you don't have sins? I don't get it. I do not think that I am a bad person and that I have sin. Everyone tells me,

'Peter, you are such a good boy. You always obey your father. They must be so proud of you. You are such a good boy."'

I believe that one of the reasons prayers of confession and the idea of repentance and contrition[3] are so rare in worship and Christian discourse today is because we, like my friend Peter, really don't think we are that bad. We live in a very affirming and supportive culture that does not want to say "no" to any behavior or attitude, at least until it becomes dangerous or expensive to others. We used to have commonly shared ideas of what was respectful public behavior and what was accepted in a marriage and in other relationships. Those common assumptions of social behavior have broken down, so it is more difficult to really see any behavior or attitude as sin or something to be confessed to God.

Either humanity is getting a lot nicer and better and there just isn't much sin any more, or our standards have slipped and we don't recognize sin as sin. Reading and listening to global news every day, I would have to say that it is the latter: our tolerance of what the Bible calls sin (and what we know by experience is sin) has changed. We put up with sinful behavior as long as it doesn't cramp our lifestyle. We, as Christians, can either coast downstream with the larger culture, or we can fight against the current and stand for something different. I believe that Christian standards for behavior (respect, forgiveness, grace, kindness, self-control) are attractive to others.

Confession and its attendant virtue, humility, are countercultural, and therefore confession becomes a signpost and a call. It is a signpost that God exists, is present, and is very personal. It is a call in that when others hear about confession, or hear "good" people confessing, that very confession becomes a call or invitation for others to humbly come before God. Without the struggle to live according to God's standards and the admission of guilt and search for mercy, we have little to offer a world being swept away by self-affirmation and greed.

Scripture gives a great example of how a higher standard can be a sign for others of God's presence and forgiveness. In one biblical case a woman becomes a sign (icon?) of God's kingdom for the Jews. One of the most genuine prayers of confession was first given as a response to

Jesus' challenge. An unnamed woman from the region of Tyre and Sidon—a Gentile—sought Jesus' attention so that he might heal her daughter. Her first words to Jesus were "Lord, Son of David, have mercy on me!" She, a non-Jew, recognized Jesus, a Son of David, as being Lord. And so she sought his mercy. Jesus, who made it clear that he came as the Messiah to the Jews (with a broader mission that would come later) ignored the pleas of the woman. She came back to him, this time kneeling, and said, "Lord, help me!" She had nothing to offer but humility and submission. Jesus, for whatever reason, made it even harder for her to be received, saying that he only came for the Jews, not for the Gentile dogs! Her response has been read all over the world and is a reminder of the extreme humility of this child of God: "Yes it is, Lord. . . . Even the dogs eat the crumbs that fall from their master's table" (Mt 15:21-28). Her remarkable response of humility has become part of a standard prayer in the global church. Beginning in 1548 the (Anglican) *Book of Common Prayer* used this same image from Matthew 15 to express what it means to come in humility before God. It is called the "Prayer of Humble Access." The following is the 1662 version:

> We do not presume to come to this thy Table, O merciful Lord, trusting in our own righteousness, but in thy manifold and great mercies. We are not worthy so much as to gather up the crumbs under thy Table. But thou art the same Lord, whose property is always to have mercy: Grant us therefore, gracious Lord, so to eat the flesh of thy dear Son Jesus Christ, and to drink his blood, that our sinful bodies may be made clean by his body, and our souls washed through his most precious blood, and that we may evermore dwell in him, and he in us. Amen.

With apologies for the sixteenth-century grammar and spelling, we see the link between confession, humility, and receiving the sacraments. Again, I am leading you to the next chapter.

REVISITING SIN AND REPENTANCE

I am reminded every time I begin to read through the Gospels, every time I read through the Old Testament stories, and every time I read Paul's and Peter's preaching in the New Testament, that sin must be dealt

with. Sin cannot be ignored. Sin cannot be pushed aside. It will come
back to bite you, and in this case, biting you can mean it will kill you.
A number of places in the Old Testament provide narrative or historical
transitions that require a literary summary section. These summary
sections always seem to have this theme:

God did all this good stuff for you.

God told you how to live and honor him.

God saved you from [the Egyptians, Philistines, etc.].

You forgot God.

You got in big trouble.

You called out to God.

God saved you.

Now, won't you remember to honor God and stop sinning?[4]

Reading through all of Scripture, this major narrative path comes back
again and again. God blesses, people thank God, they forget what God
has done and take matters into their own hands, and everything gets
messed up: families divide, wars with neighbors begin, blessings are
removed, and eventually all of God's family is conquered and sent into
exile. Then we read something like this: "Then they cried out to the LORD
and said, 'We have sinned; we have forsaken the LORD and served the
Baals and the Ashtoreths. But now deliver us from the hands of our
enemies, and we will serve you'" (1 Sam 12:10).

Confession and repentance are the signs of both the beginning of life
through Jesus Christ and ongoing life with Jesus. This is central to life:
admitting failure and inability to correct things. Surrender is the pathway
to blessings and joy. There is no other way.

However, we live in societies that decry confession as weakness, not
seeing it as a virtue. Our heroes are designed and molded by the media
to have no flaws. Even in our pre-adolescent and adolescent cultures we
allow the strong to dominate the weak, the honest confessors to be dominated by the dishonest powerful. All of this is a lie. But it is our culture,
our context, our environment.

In contrast, as Christians, we know that confession opens a beautiful
and life-giving path to God. There is no other way to have fullness of life

and healthy relationships with God and with others. We can bring nothing—nada, zero, zip, zilch, aught, zippo—to God. When we do try to win God's acceptance, we cannot be fully in God's presence. Only with empty hands can we receive what God offers to us.

It is frightening to be completely empty and naked before God. We do not want to be exposed. It is a great irony that all that we bring to God is nothing . . . well, nothing except a false sense of security. God is not impressed with what we bring. Only our surrender moves him. In confession, we surrender, and in surrender we find out that we receive more than we ever imagined or dreamed. The pain and sorrow of confession is met with the joy of true relationship, with love, for God is love.

And this leads us to the joy and power of confession. After we have confessed and turned the reins of our life back to a powerful, merciful, and gentle God, we are in position to receive. Hands empty, soul cleansed, we can receive the power of God's grace for others. We often forget that confession is not personal therapy (although it is a necessary element of personal wholeness); it prepares us to serve others. Everything God gives us—his calling, cleansing, joy, gifts, and talents—all is given to us *to serve others.*

God does not call us to leave us; he calls us to send us. And confession is one of two necessary moves that prepare us to be sent. The other is to receive from God. Emptied of sin, we are prepared to receive before being sent. Now we sit.

AND WHAT HAPPENED TO PETER?

It seemed impossible to convince Peter that he needed a savior if he was without sin. It is no fun to try to convince someone that they are a sinner when you know that they seem very nice on the outside. Everyone loved Peter. He was a joy to be around, and he was very bright. So I simply prayed that somehow he would know his need for Jesus even if others told him that he was not in need of a savior.

One day, about four months later, Peter came into my office, sat down and confidently announced, "I am a Christian." After quietly fixing him a cup of tea and praying under my breath ("Lord help me to say the right thing. Don't let me blow it!") I asked him, "Tell me how this happened." It was fairly simple. The very evangelistic pastor of the Chinese church asked Peter to work the overhead projector (before PowerPoint) that projected the words of the hymns and songs onto the screen. Thus, he was looking down at every word and learning to sing songs of praise. As he told me that day, "When I looked at those words, I was over- whelmed at how wonderful and loving God is. I knew that I could never live up to God's standards. I knew, as I came to know God through the songs, that I was a sinner."

There you go. In the presence of such a great (and good) loving God, we know our need for confession and forgiveness. But all of this depends on our knowing God better each day.

6

SIT

IT SEEMS THAT FOR MANY CHRISTIANS in the world, at least for many Protestant Christians, church is about preaching. People like to go to a
worship service and even join a church where there is "good preaching."
Many people have told me (in fact, I have myself said), "We are looking
for a church where there is good preaching."[1] This is not a new thing at
all. In the latter part of the nineteenth century a young preacher, a
convert to the Baptist church, began preaching to larger and larger congregations until he ended up in a building that seated 5,600 people: the
Metropolitan Tabernacle. His sermons were printed every Monday
morning in the *London Times* and even in the *New York Times*, on both
sides of the Atlantic. People loved to hear and even read his sermons. For
thousands of people the sermons of Charles Spurgeon (1834–1892) were
the reason for going to church.

For many people, going to a particular church is still voting for the
best communicator; we say "communicator" because all "great preachers"
do not necessarily proclaim accurate, healthy, and helpful gospel messages. Good music also attracts people today, as if the quality of the
music is an indication of the value of the worship—or at least of the
praise. But good music, like good preaching, can be shallow and non-
nutritious. Like empty calories, they do not nourish the soul. "Religion"
is a false substitute for salvation through Jesus Christ, and empty rhetoric
can be just words without the Word. Whether the preaching, the music,
the community, or the community outreach attracts people, we talk
about all of these in order to remind us that we can be attracted to an
element of a church that is more attractive than spiritual, more exciting

than Christian. We seek not a show or even preaching from worldly wisdom, but proclamation in the church of "Christ the power of God and the wisdom of God" (1 Cor 1:24).

This chapter discusses how we get up from our knees (confession) to sit and receive from God. In worship we receive more than one thing. We receive the Word read. We also receive the Word preached or proclaimed. We will see that the Word proclaimed today may include other modes of communication: art, dance, video, and multimedia presentations. Finally, we receive the elements of the body of Christ during this period of worship. Receiving is not only possible but necessary once we have emptied ourselves in humble confession. We empty ourselves of our sin because Jesus tells us to; he can absorb or take our sin upon himself. Now with the poisons and garbage of our sinfulness emptied, there is room for the good and nourishing and true. We feed on Jesus and his Word.

RECEIVING THE WORD READ

I think it is hard for people to sit still in the twenty-first century and hear someone read out loud to them. There are so many distractions. I remember when we lived in Singapore (in the days before Netflix and Amazon Prime), we had three TV stations that had programming in four languages: Tamil, Mandarin, Malay, and English. The choice was very limited and not very inviting. We were not tempted to spend the evening watching TV. So in the evenings we dealt with our culture shock by reading good books (mostly funny) from the West. At that time, with little else to do in the evening, our entertainment was reading. I would read a chapter and then my wife would read a chapter. We would laugh and laugh, picturing the stories as they were told. And then we would sleep.

Today, it is hard for people to just listen to words being read out loud. Our hypervisual culture, with movies and video clips on our computers, phones, and even billboards, make it hard for us, as a community, to just sit and listen to a voice. However, our hypervisual culture is no reason to assume people cannot listen to something read or an oral presentation. A good oral presentation still is engaging, and it can be transformative.

We listen to TED Talks, stand-up comedians, audio books, and some-times we listen to politicians.

Let me explain the importance of listening to Scripture read in two ways, one historical and one very personal. In the early church—in fact, until the common use of moveable type in the seventeenth century[2]—people learned about the Bible by listening to it being read. In the first years after the resurrection of Jesus, Paul's letters (as well as the Gospels and Acts) were read to people in villages or communities. Except for a very few who had the time (and the materials) to copy the letters, everyone knew about Jesus and Paul's instructions about following Jesus by hearing a letter read out loud to a small community. Christian discipleship was a matter of speaking and hearing and then doing. Until, and even through the sixteenth-century Protestant Refor-mation, almost everyone depended on the oral communication of the gospel. Artwork—stained glass windows, statues, frescos—reinforced the stories and other readings.

If this were the case for most of the history of the church, we should be very respectful of the simple oral presentation of Scripture today. Not only does this continue to be important, but we also believe that reading Scripture, publically or corporately, has power. Scripture is not just human interpretations of some historical events in a far-off corner of the world. Scripture—the Bible we read from our phones, our computers, or in a book held in our hand—is God's Word to us. Peter says something very interesting about the Old Testament prophets.

> Concerning this salvation, the prophets, who spoke of the grace that was to come to you, searched intently and with the greatest care, trying to find out the time and circumstances to which the Spirit of Christ in them was pointing when he predicted the sufferings of the Messiah and the glories that would follow. It was revealed to them that they were not serving themselves but you, when they spoke of the things that have now been told you by those who have preached the gospel to you by the Holy Spirit sent from heaven. Even angels long to look into these things. (1 Pet 1:10-12)

This amazing passage indicates that the prophets of the Old Testament—in this case I think he is referring to Isaiah—were aware that the Holy Spirit was guiding them as to what to write and say. The Holy Spirit gave them the key to understanding the identity of the Messiah. The Messiah, the anointed one of God, is the one who will suffer (the cross) and then be received in glory (resurrection and ascension). God's Word, certainly the words of the Old Testament, is inspired by God's Holy Spirit. We should listen to them! Paul says something similar: "All Scripture is God-breathed" (2 Tim 3:16). Just hearing Scripture read can have power; it comes from God's Holy Spirit and can be applied to our souls by that same Spirit of God.

My second reason for the oral reading of Scripture is more personal. I have a number of grandchildren (ten at last count), and we love to do two things when we visit them. First, I like to take them out to get donuts. It has become a type of ritual. "Grandpa is here! The donut man!" Our other ritual is reading books. From the very earliest time children can listen to any human communication, they love to sit on the couch and hear a good story. In the early stages they are making connections between the pictures and the words, learning to visualize the story by looking at an artist's version of the words. Later, the pictures are not so important. They will listen for a long time to a good story (often longer than I want to read). This is why most children's story Bibles are just that, books that tell the stories of the Bible. Children have a hard time with the instructional or pedagogical passages, but they remember Noah and the Ark; they can tell the story of David and Goliath; and many remember Elijah tired and depressed being fed by the ravens. And of course they remember Jesus healing the blind man and feeding the people. They remember these stories—stories read out loud to a small group.

In fact, I remember when our children were very young (2, 4, 6, and 8) they went forward for the children's sermon in church. The pastor thought he was telling the story about Paul for the first time for the children. However, when he told about Paul's conversion, our four-year-old blurted out: "His name was Saul! Then it was changed to Paul when Jesus came to him!" Well, someone had been listening to Bible stories.

We should listen to the reading of Scripture expectantly. Be prepared to be captured by the Word, to be confronted, or to be comforted. This is as it should be. God's Word is "alive and active. Sharper than any double-edged sword, it penetrates even to dividing soul and spirit, joints and marrow; it judges the thoughts and attitudes of the heart" (Heb 4:12). This being the case, the reading of the Bible should be done well and marinated with prayer.

Although a sermon may focus on a single verse of Scripture, it is best to read larger passages so everyone can hear more rather than less of the Bible each week. Most Christian traditions have an Old Testament reading (sometimes a Psalm) and a Gospel reading and a reading from the letters. This encourages the congregation to be discipled or guided by all of the Bible rather than being guided by the few favorite passages or books that the pastor likes to preach from. Reading from many places in the Bible helps to ensure that Scripture will speak to the many issues in a congregation's life; it will raise a variety of important questions that people need to think about. It is quite OK to listen to a whole story from the Old Testament, a complete psalm (well, maybe not Psalm 119), a Gospel reading, and a reading from Paul, John, or Peter. It really doesn't take as long as we think, and it will help to prevent shallowness in our Christian life. But the Bible should be read well. Then allow the preacher to explain part of the reading further.

RECEIVING THE WORD PROCLAIMED

Next, as it was done in the synagogues of Jesus' time, the rabbi (teacher) explains the passage. The explanation (sermon, homily, preaching) is not merely theoretical; its purpose is to help the hearers to live into the passage. As the Word is proclaimed it should become evident what the passage means for the mother with young children, the adolescent soccer player, the retired mechanic, the schoolteacher, and the unemployed salesman. Preaching, or explaining the Bible to a congregation, is not an easy task. It takes much time and prayer to take a passage and lift it up to God to be blessed for a particular community of Jesus followers. It is wonderful when done well. It is a crime when done flippantly or with little attention to both the Word and the people. As Christians listening to the message, we need to be aware of the weight of responsibility that it is to deliver a message from God to a diverse community of folks eager to receive a Word from God.

What exactly is happening in preaching? In preaching God's very Word, the Word (that brought about all of creation) is doing a re-creating in the lives of the church members. It is a sacred and powerful event (for it is an event). Paul is concerned in 1 Corinthians that many people who are more concerned for their names proclaim a message with no power, just a lot of show. He talks about those who proclaim the good news with "eloquence or human wisdom" and contrasts this with the clear proclamation of "Jesus Christ and him crucified" (1 Cor 2:1-2). Paul's clear and simple message, he claims, has power through the "Spirit that is from God" (1 Cor 2:12). In proclaiming the good news, the message must focus on Jesus Christ; we pray that there will be a "demonstration of the Spirit and of power" (1 Cor 2:4). Proclaiming the message from God is no little thing. The one proclaiming is playing with dynamite (*dynamis* is Greek for "power").

Preaching to each and every one. I remember many years ago when we would go to worship, we struggled to sit through a service together because our children were young: two and four years old. We were perpetually tired, and we really needed a good word from the Lord. One Sunday after the sermon Nancy turned to me and said something like this: "That was so helpful. The pastor preaches as if he is counseling me with the Bible." I find that a helpful description of preaching. Preaching applies the words of God to our soul: "Wonderful Counselor" was one of the designations of Jesus ("Mighty God, Everlasting Father, Prince of Peace," Is 9:6).

When it comes time for the sermon, we should expect the message to be for us, personally and even intimately. We have just confessed our sins, so we should be aware of our need for a word from God.[3] We may not be personally known by the preacher; in fact, we may not even be seen by the preacher, but that is not the point. The point is that preaching is a divine moment when the Holy Spirit is alive and active in applying God's Word to us as individuals.

I learned this lesson very clearly when I was studying preaching in seminary. We had just finished a three-hour class, and I was quite aware that our first attempts at preaching were not really that scintillating. In fact, I bored myself with my first sermon. I was much too self-conscious trying to follow the guidelines of the professor. So walking up the hill to the cafeteria I looked over at the godly and long-suffering servant of a professor, Gwyn Walters, and said, "You have a difficult job. I can't imagine listening to these student sermons day in and day out as you have for so many years. How do you do it?" His response caught me completely off-guard: "Oh, no, Scott. You are wrong. I count it such a privilege to get to hear God's Word preached every day I am on campus. What an honor it is. In every sermon I learn a little something new. Sometimes I am really surprised, but in every sermon God teaches me something."

And if that is true for someone who listens to hundreds of sermons a month, then there is something for us in each sermon we listen to. God meets us as individuals. He speaks to you, to me in our particular situation in life.

But God also speaks to all of us, to everyone as a congregation, when the Word is preached. The local church, as a local representation of the body of Christ, listens to preaching as a community. There is always something for *us*, even as there is something for *me*. Therefore, we also need to listen as a community to what is preached. What does this say to us as we live out our lives following Jesus in our part of the city or in our town? So we listen for what is said to us as a community called to be the presence of Christ in a particular place at this particular time.

This is a very important word regarding the church. Paul wrote letters to individuals (Timothy, Titus), and he wrote letters to congregations identified in local communities (Romans, Corinthians, Ephesians, Philippians, Colossians, Thessalonians). God speaks to congregations, often to the surprise of the preacher, about gossip, truth-telling, anger issues, care for the poor in the neighborhood, and building stronger marriages. The preacher doesn't need to fine-tune his sermon as if sharpening a spear for an attack on particular vices. No, in fact, if the preacher faithfully lifts up God's Word, the Holy Spirit will apply the teaching to areas of sin as well as to areas of woundedness in the congregation. When we are attentive to the sermon, we are ready for a personal word and for a word to our community. We ask both, "What is God saying to me?" and "What is God saying to us?"

Scripture interpreting Scripture. An active and attentive church member will listen to a particular sermon about a particular passage and begin to make connections with other passages of Scripture. From week to week as the congregation gathers to hear the Word read and preached, they deepen their life story into the story of Scripture. This means that hearing a sermon on a particular passage should lead us to make connections with other passages throughout Scripture. Although much of our modern study of the Bible in universities and seminaries analyze, dissect, and take apart Scripture, we have from Jesus, John, Peter, and Paul examples that show that the best preaching understands Scripture as a whole. A sermon on Jesus' Sermon on the Mount should lead us to think about how these teachings are both new but also (as Jesus said) a fulfillment of the Law. "Blessed are the poor" is a clear teaching that has already been given to Israel of old. "If you lend money to one of my people among you who is needy, do not treat it like a business deal; charge no interest" (Ex 22:25). The Old Testament says many, many things about treatment and care of the poor. "When you reap the harvest of your land, do not reap to the very edges of your field or gather the gleanings of your harvest. Leave them for the poor and for the foreigner residing among you. I am the LORD your God" (Lev 23:22). And to make even clearer the importance of caring for the poor, we read in Proverbs 19:17: "Whoever is kind to the poor lends to the LORD." Scripture interprets Scripture, clarifying our calling in life.

> We ask both, "What is God saying to me?" and "What is God saying to us?"

This is true of every passage and every teaching in the Bible. Scripture is wonderfully interwoven, self-interpreting, vibrant, and fertile. If we hear a sermon on marriage from Ephesians, we can also find teachings on marriage from the Law, from Jesus, and even from Song of Songs! Truth-telling, deception, pride, sacrifice, holiness are all found throughout the Bible. Rather than a one-time, late-night television special, preaching is more like an ongoing series that connects the stories and life of the Bible with our lives and the life of the congregation. This point leads to two other issues related to sermons.

Memorizing passages. I am going out on a limb a bit here, but I want to pause to think again of the value and the power of Scripture to bring about transformation in our lives. After we hear a good sermon, it is good if we can share what we learned with others. It is helpful to remember the message and the main concerns of the passage. I would suggest, however, that it is of even greater value to remember the Bible passage or passages. Good preaching should bring before us the great passages that should become part of our lives. If the passage is in our head, it can soften our heart and direct our hands.

> If the passage is in our head, it can soften our heart and direct our hands.

Before literacy was so common (and now social media), people memorized stories, poetry, and passages. What you have in your mind makes it possible to think with your mind. We can think with the mind of Christ (1 Cor 2:16; Phil 2:5) when we have the words of Christ in our mind. As a covenant community, the church is the place where we can speak the very words of God to each other and begin to see lives changed. It is so much better to avoid saying, "Well, it says somewhere in the Bible; let me do a quick Google search . . ." and to say instead: "Remember, 'God did not give us a spirit of cowardice, but rather a spirit of power and of love and of self-discipline'" (2 Tim 1:7 NRSV). Memorizing Scripture, especially Scripture that has spoken to us from a sermon, helps in our transformation and in the flourishing of a local church community.

Church calendar. Many churches integrate the teachings of the whole Bible by following a basic plan for reading through the main stories of Scripture throughout the Christian year. Some of the people reading this section will be thinking, *Of course, that is what you do; you follow the lectionary readings.* Others of you are thinking, *What? You mean you read the same passages every year? Who decided that and what is a lectionary?*

There are many different lectionary reading plans, but all of them have the purpose of guiding the church through the basic message of the Bible, from creation to the new creation, every year. Most follow the church calendar starting with Advent, or the announcement of the coming of the Messiah (late November), going through Christmas time (which is more than just Christmas Day!), Epiphany (twelve days after Christmas) through Lent, Easter, and what is called ordinary time. Church calendars mark important events in Scripture as well as in Christian history through the celebration of feasts and fasts.

We bring up this tradition simply to say that following the church calendar and the lectionary readings is one way to make sure that all of Scripture and most of the major themes in Scripture are heard from the pulpit.[4]

Sermons are not . . . I was amazed, when in seminary many decades ago, to read a long introduction to a seventeenth-century book. The introduction was so long that it became its own book and is still in print. If a book is still in print after 350 years, there might be something significant for us today. The book is by Philip Jacob Spener: *Pia Desideria*, or *Pious Desires* (longings). This book calls for reforms in the church that will bring about greater piety (devotion) among Christians in Germany. I was amazed to read it because I thought, "Oh, my! This is still true today. Spener could have written this book last year!"

One of the reforms Spener called for helps us see what preaching is not. After talking about the "defects"[5] in the clergy and the defects in the laity, he writes about "proposals to correct conditions in the church." The first proposal is, "Thought should be given to a more extensive use of the Word of God among us." In explaining this concern about the knowledge and application of Scripture, his sixth and last point speaks to seminary students getting ready to preach.

> Everything in their sermons should have edification as their goal. . . .
> [S]ermons should be so prepared by all that their purpose (faith and its fruits)
> may be achieved in the hearers to the greatest possible degree. . . . There are
> probably few places in our church in which there is such a want that not
> enough sermons are preached. But many godly persons find that not a little

is wanting in many sermons. There are preachers who fill most of their sermons with things that give the impression that the preachers are learned [folks], although the hearers understand nothing of this.[6]

Whether in the seventeenth century or this week, sermons are not a time for the preacher to show off her or his learning or rhetorical skills. Preaching is in service to the congregation and to any guests who may be present. These kinds of sermons are memorable and powerful. Sermons that make the preacher look sharp and smart are forgettable and powerless. Rather than complaining when we hear a preacher falling into this error, we need to pray for our preachers. The work is hard, because the power of preaching comes from hard work and conscious self-emptying. Preachers need our prayers.

In summary, sermons speak to each of us and to all of us. We need to dwell in Scripture and have it nourish our souls as a result of the preaching event. We will be challenged by Scripture (because we are sinners) and we will also be comforted (because we are broken). We don't want to respond to the sermon by saying, "Wow, what a kind and thoughtful pastor," but "Yes, that is true, Jesus is the Lord and the shepherd of our souls. He will take care of us." Such preaching comes from the Word and speaks to the people, guiding, comforting, and (at times) disturbing us in our sin.

The preacher is the mouthpiece and messenger, not to be confused with the message itself. For the preacher to be the focus is malpractice. Sermons are not the time to grandstand.

RECEIVING THE BODY OF CHRIST

When we are sitting, we receive the Word read or recited. We also receive the Word explained, proclaimed, or preached. Finally, when seated, we also receive Jesus, the Word made flesh, in a tangible way.[7] Most Christians in the world recognize the celebration of the Lord's Supper (the Eucharist or Communion) not only as an important element of Christian community life, but also as a sacrament.[8] The Lord's Supper unites Christians throughout all of time and in all places and focuses our worship and meditation on Jesus Christ. Unfortunately, it also divides

Christians because of the ways it is practiced and understood. Even though the practice of the Lord's Supper is often divisive, we focus here on its place in the life of the whole Church as it is practiced in a local church. We will spend very little time on ways that the Lord's Supper has been divisive and focus instead on how it unites and guides the church more deeply into Jesus Christ. It is called "the Lord's Supper" because our Lord established it, and it points to the meaning of the Lord's life and death (Mt 26:17-30; Lk 22:7-23). We want to focus on this. Throughout the history of Christianity, the Lord's Supper has been a consistent practice that sets Christians apart as "people of the meal."

The meaning of the Lord's Supper lies in the story of Jesus' life. This special Passover meal of Jesus comes at the climax of the story of his life, and as the climax, it is the focal point. Let's step back and think about Jesus' life and the place of the Lord's Supper in the whole narrative.

Jesus' birth is described as a miracle or pure birth, a birth of a child when Mary had not even had intercourse with a man. The birth of Jesus, as well as the birth of his cousin, John the Baptist, is celebrated as a great and epoch-making event where creation (the star and animals) is witness, and angels sing for joy (Lk 2:8-20). But the narrative also includes the foreboding story of the political powers feeling threatened by this birth and so seeking to stop this glorious beginning before it gets very far. Herod slaughters infants and children in an effort to silence the special messenger before he can speak. He survives as a refugee in Egypt, returns, and soon we find out that he is more than a messenger. He came to bring a message, exhibit something of the kingdom of God, and to be the fulfillment of God's Law. In his travels he speaks, performs miracles, fore-tells the future, and casts out demons. It is quite a show, really. However, Jesus seems to reduce the size of the crowd following him with some hard teachings in an effort to make sure his followers are genuine followers and not just thrill seekers (Jn 6:52-66).

Jesus and his message convey a finality. His message also indicates a genesis. He is bringing the end to something tragic, and he is beginning something glorious. Slowly, as the stories unfold, we find out that this is more than just a local tribal wonderworker; this is something much more cosmic and magnificent. After gathering many followers—people who will do almost anything to be in his presence or to touch his clothes—he enters triumphant into Jerusalem, the City of God. It is a victorious parade to the religious center of the Jews.

But the climax and dénouement of the story turn out not at all as expected. We had earlier warnings of a surprise ending, and Jesus certainly knew what would happen, but what happened caught everyone (except for the protagonist) by complete surprise. And this is why the Lord's Supper has a central place. When all seems to be wonderful, when Jesus is being celebrated as a hero, he unexpectedly calls his closest companions together and shows them what his whole life is about, and what our lives are about. It is not what they thought. It is not just a victory parade. Jesus makes it clear that he did not come to live, but to die. The diagnosis of the human condition is far worse than they thought. We do not just need teaching, some correction, and healing. We are not simply in error and sick; we are dead wrong. In fact, we are dead. Death can only be conquered by the death of one who is pure: immaculate. And so at the Lord's Supper, Jesus announces that he will do what no one else can do, but what everyone needs to be done. He will voluntarily give up his life so that we can live.

Jesus is not just the good news,[9] he is also the good work. And so we can only live if we live off of the life and death of Jesus. "This is my body given for you. . . . This cup is the new covenant in my blood, which is poured out for you" (Lk 22:19-20). Jesus is a prophet, but in this Passover meal, the world learned that he is also the sacrificial lamb. After making this announcement and sealing it with a symbolic, even mystical, meal, he takes up his cross and invites us to follow him.

This is why I say that the Lord's Supper is the climax of the story of Jesus, which is also the story of redemption for all of the world. After this sacred meal come the crucifixion, death, burial, and then the second big surprise: the resurrection. Without the first surprise (Jesus accepted his premature death), there would be no second (and necessary) surprise: the conquest of death. The climax gives sense to the surprising dénouement (resurrection). Jesus commands us to remember him in this special way, by repeating this ceremony, this sacrament, this remembering over and over again. We need to remember the core, the foundation, the climax of the story of life. But what are we really doing when we rehearse again and again the Lord's Supper?

The Lord's Supper is the Eucharist is Holy Communion. On a few occasions I have visited a church and asked, "Do you celebrate Communion today?" and was corrected, "Oh, I am sorry, we call it Eucharist." The many names of this special meal have reasons. Calling it the Lord's Supper follows the way Paul talked about it when he gave instructions in 1 Corinthians 11. It is the supper instituted *by* our Lord and the supper *of* our Lord. It is all about Jesus, who gave his life so we could have life. In no way does this meal belong to a church, a denomination, a person, or a country. It is the Lord's Supper where we, in some mystical way, eat the flesh and drink the blood of Jesus (John 6), who is our life. Jesus is the host and we—all Christians united—are the guests.

But it is also a meal of thanksgiving. *Eucharisteō* means "I give thanks"; *euchariste* is the command "Give thanks!" In this meal we remember that Jesus gave up his glory and communion with the Father to show us the love of God and to pay the penalty for our sins. Every week we celebrate this, and we express again and again our thanksgiving to Jesus for the work he has done for us. His obedience and suffering to the extent of death for us has given us the great benefits we still share and continue to enjoy each day. As a reminder, we have said that the foundation of worship—in fact, the foundation of the Christian life—is thanksgiving. The name Eucharist makes perfect sense for a core sacrament that we celebrate each week (hopefully).[10]

Finally, this meal brings us into communion with God and with each other. The Communion meal is a meal that Jesus shared with his disciples; it is a meal that unites us to God, and it is the meal that we always share together as the children of God, the Church of Jesus Christ. The Church—the body of Christ—is united in the meal where we share in the body of Christ. It is an interesting double-entendre. In communing together we all come as people who are repentant (kneel), empty, with hands open and extended. Everyone is equal before Jesus and his cross of suffering. This leads us to a quick look at the cosmic vision of the Eucharist.

Eucharistic vision. On a number of occasions I have had insight into the power of the Eucharist. Although we are talking in this volume about receiving the body and blood of Jesus sitting, many traditions have rails (often kneeling rails) at the front of the church where people come forward to receive the elements with their hands open, with one palm on top of the other at a 90-degree angle. Hands are in the sign of a cross. If there is no rail, people get up from their pews or seats and walk forward in a long line of sinners seeking grace. And here priests, pastors, and lay leaders who serve Communion all share a remarkable vision.

The congregation comes forward, slowly, deliberately, and in an attitude of contrition. Everyone comes forward who has, at one point in his or her life, said something like, "I give up, God. Please, you take my life and save it and give me new life."[11] When I stand up in the front of the church, by the table, with the cup or the plate of bread (representing Jesus' death for us), I see everyone come forward. Wealthy men and women in fine clothes and expensive-smelling perfume. Children come with their parents, and the elderly are helped forward by friends or by their children. Some come with walkers or even in wheel chairs. Young adolescent athletes, who are usually the center of attention in their high school, come humbly and quietly in need. The new immigrants from Syria, Guatemala, or Iraq come forward with the conservative patriot who is not sure refugees should come to the United States. People of all races, classes, employment, and age, even people of all mental abilities come together. Homeless people who have slept on the steps of the church and wealthy church leaders and business executives are all equal and equally needy before the cross. It is a vision of Jesus as Lord of life and of all the nations of the world coming to receive life from him alone. Communion is a sign of the Great Banquet. This is the Church. There is no community like it in all of the world and in all of history.

INTERMISSION: BAPTISM

Presentations about the church usually keep sacraments together, and thus we will do so here. We just spoke about the Lord's Supper, Communion, or the Eucharist with a brief mention that most every church in the world considers it a sacrament. *Sacrament* comes from the Latin word for "mystery" (*mystērion* in Greek). So what is the mystery? From as early as the fourth or fifth century the church has commonly accepted a definition of sacrament: an outward sign of an inward grace initiated by Jesus Christ. As with all of worship, but especially with sacraments, a spiritual work takes place, even if we are not aware of it. Worship and certainly the sacraments are not play-acting. In baptism, as with the Lord's Supper, we are doing what Jesus commanded us to do (Mt 28:19), and what has been the pattern from the very beginning of the church. The earliest Christian history book of Acts shows the pattern clearly: people believed and were baptized (Acts 2:37-41; 8:5-13, 36-38; 9:17-19, among others).

In a country where many or most people are Christian, baptism may not seem to be so remarkable. But it is. What does baptism mean? Let me explain baptism with four words:

1. Alive (rather than dead!)

2. Cleansed (of sin and all its disease and stain)

3. Enlisted (on the side of Jesus and the angels)

4. Enfolded (into Jesus Christ)

The Bible uses many images to explain baptism, but rather than going through all of the passages and inferences about baptism (such as the Israelites going through the Red Sea), I find these four words helpful in thinking about the meaning of baptism. As a mystery (sacrament), more than one thing is going on when we baptize someone. First, baptism symbolizes that we have gone from death to life. Sin kills us. Sin separates us from God and therefore we are dead. In baptism we come alive to God in Christ. Baptism symbolizes this by full immersion where the person goes down into the waters (symbolizing the grave) and then rises out of the waters (symbolizing resurrection).

Second, baptism symbolizes our being cleansed of sin and its stain. Actually, it is more than a stain; the results of sin are more like an indelible stain or even a disease. For this reason, many traditions pour water over the infant or adult at baptism, symbolizing the cleansing that takes place through Christ. This is the initial cleansing of sin and its result: death. However, cleansing occurs again and again after baptism when we confess our sins and turn these stains over to Christ who willingly receives them. Pouring water over the head of an infant or adult in symbolic cleansing supports the argument for using more rather than less water at baptism: to preserve the meaning of cleansing.

Third, baptism is like enlisting a person in a cosmic battle. In many traditions the infant or candidate for baptism has the sign of the cross marked on their forehead. I think it is a great idea, both for the person being baptized and for the congregation to be reminded that they are marked for Jesus and marked for battle. This is a way of telling the demons, "Back off. I belong to one who is far more powerful than you. I am marked by baptism and enrolled in the kingdom of God." In many cultures baptism is very contentious or even dangerous. If you are the only one in the village or in the family who has become Christian, your baptism is a way of saying, "I now belong to Jesus, not to my religious family of origin." Many people throughout the history of the church, and even today, are being killed or they become refugees from their home because they are baptized.

Baptism is cosmic, not just personal, and certainly not private.

Finally, baptism says something about our identity and power. Before baptism I may have lived for myself and by myself, finding meaning in the little things I worshiped. But now I am identified with Jesus in his body, participating in his mission in this world. I have joined a community called the church with accountability for others, with people looking out for me, and with a common call to the world. One of the first verses I memorized has come back to me as I write this paragraph: "I have been crucified with Christ and I no longer live, but Christ lives in me. The life I now live in the body, I live by faith in the Son of God, who loved me and gave himself for me" (Gal 2:20). Baptism is a sign that we have a new identity. But it is more than a sign. It is a sign that points to a reality. I really do have a new identity and a new purpose in life. With baptism, the journey begins.

Infants or believers? I will not solve the age-old controversy over baptizing infants or only believers who have come to an age of accountability.[12] Here I will only give the reason *for* each of the two practices. Baptizing infants expresses the confidence that God has always (and normatively) called families not individuals to faith. God has always worked through families and he continues to do so. Therefore, we see in Scripture that when Lydia came to faith, she and her household were all baptized (Acts 16:13-15). Did they all have the same conversion experience that Lydia had? Scripture does not indicate they did. God works through families, so in the normal pattern Christian parents baptize their children, and in countries where a family may have workers living with them, they bring them all to worship. Infant baptism assumes the normal pattern of God's kingdom works through families. Of course this also assumes that baptism is connected with a Christian community, worship, teachings, and Christian care. Baptism initiates into the life in Christ. It is commencement as beginning not as graduation!

Those who assume the norm of believer's baptism or adult baptism see Paul or the Ethiopian eunuch as the norm (Acts 8:26-39; 9:1-19). An individual alone comes to faith and is baptized. Therefore, after conversion, when a child or adult confesses that he or she trusts their life to Jesus Christ, the person should be baptized. Believer's baptism assumes a person has just received God's grace and so was not baptized as an infant. Children in Christian homes are assumed to need to make their own decision to give their life to Christ, and so there are concerted efforts to make sure all children make a profession of faith and are baptized publicly. Many churches today allow for both types of baptism (or baptism and dedication).

Both those who baptize infants as part of the Christian family and those who only baptize confessing young people or adults believe that

Christian families should worship together and that children should be under the instruction of the church. Many, if not most, of those who baptize believers will dedicate infants or young children in a worship service as a way of saying, "This child is dedicated to Jesus Christ and will someday confess for herself that she is trusting her life to Jesus."

I hope not to create too much division here, so let's look at a few obvious truths upon which we can agree. Many people who are baptized cannot bring their whole family to church or to faith in Christ. When a college student from a Buddhist home comes to faith, it may be years before the rest of the family comes to Jesus. Therefore, they may wait a while, but eventually they wish to be fully part of a church and so they will submit to baptism alone. Many Muslims coming to faith in Jesus Christ live in communities that react violently to Christian baptism. Thus, many Muslim-background believers are secretly baptized or resist baptism until more in their Muslim community come to follow Isa (Jesus).

The majority of the Christians in the world (Roman Catholic, Orthodox, Methodist, Anglican, Lutheran, Presbyterian, etc. represent over two-thirds of all Christians) baptize infants under the assumption that the family is part of God's kingdom. Most of these children will affirm the faith for themselves later (called confirmation), but many will not see their life as "before I was a Christian and then after I came to faith."

The particular practices of baptism as well as of Eucharist vary according to church tradition and cultural context. I have celebrated the Eucharist with sticky rice and with Ribena juice, wine, port, tea, leavened bread, unleavened bread (crackers), and with really delicious homemade and whole wheat bread (all natural). I have seen baptisms in a small portable pool in a sanctuary, in a large tank with steps down into the water, in swimming pools, lakes, and with water poured over a head, and little drops dropped on an infant's head. I have seen Orthodox infants dunked in a large baptismal font. I have my preferences, but I am actually very little concerned that my preference is known or taught.

These practices point to the same reality: a work of divine grace, or unmerited transforming grace, is actually taking place. We should be in awe.

Who can bless water and wine? The sacraments of baptism and Eucharist both involve the community and point to Jesus. We might ask why anyone can't just baptize whomever they want, and why just anyone can't celebrate the Lord's Supper. Can't families have their little Eucharist ceremonies at home? A little history may be helpful to understand why the church sets aside only some people to lead (celebrate) sacraments. As with much history, when we don't understand it, we may (probably will) make the same mistakes in the future. There is no reason to glory in ignorance.

In the earliest church one of the most significant questions that repeatedly came up had to do with authority. When Jesus was alive, his followers (and potential followers) asked him questions. Jesus was the authority. When he was gone, who would you ask? Well, Paul appealed to the authority that he had as one who had encountered the risen Christ directly (Gal 1), and others said simply only those who had been with Jesus could speak with authority. Thus, an early letter to the Corinthians from Clement in Rome (97 CE) was actually considered as Holy Scripture by some early Christians. Trust those close to Jesus and their followers.

But when these people became old and died, how would you know what Jesus actually said? There were two basic answers: you could trust the tradition that was passed down from person to person (called apostolic succession), or you could trust the writings from those who had been with Jesus. If Paul had spoken to Titus and Timothy, then you could trust the teaching from these folks. If a later person, like Clement, Polycarp (69–155), or Irenaeus (d. 202) taught about Jesus and we can trace that they learned from someone who learned from John the apostle or from Paul, then their teaching could be trusted. This is when Scriptures and the idea of a pope as the final authority both developed as answers to the question of authority. The popes were understood to be in a direct line with Jesus (followed by Peter and then Linus and Anacletus and Clement I, and so on).

As today, the need to answer the question of authority arose because people began to teach ideas similar to what Jesus taught, but with a twist. Some said that Jesus was not really God, but he was the best prophet. Others said he was God, but he was not really human. Some said that Jesus' real teachings were secret and only if you had the secret teachings could you reach immortality. Various leaders taught all types of ideas about what Jesus taught, and it got very confusing. Some taught that there were secret teachings to the Eucharist. Today, some very influential pastors begin to say things that sound a little eccentric. So, who can you trust? How can you know for sure?

Two places where the core teachings of Jesus were protected were around baptism and the Lord's Supper. These embodied the core teachings of the life and death of Jesus, the foundation of the kingdom of God. Here lies the importance of ensuring that the person celebrating the sacraments is following the teachings of Jesus and of Paul and Peter and of the Great Tradition of the Church that followed them. The teachings and practice can be protected in many ways, but the most obvious way is to have some basic teachings, confessions, practices that will be passed on to people set aside to oversee the sacraments. This aligns with the Old Testament practice of having a priestly class to oversee worship in the temple and with Paul's concern to pass on the correct teachings of Jesus. Paul called these people overseers.[13] One of the people Paul entrusted with responsibility to oversee churches was the much-younger Timothy. He said to Timothy, "The things you have heard from me say in the presence of many witnesses entrust to reliable people who will also be qualified to teach others" (2 Tim 2:2). The second letter of John also shows the concern to protect the teachings about Jesus.

Setting aside certain persons to oversee the preaching, teaching, and exercise of the sacraments has been the consistent practice of the Church from the beginning. Whether this is the same person or persons or different persons, whether the person is elected or selected through an agreed upon process differs among churches and across time. The important concern is that the church does take care to

ensure that the preaching of the Word and leadership in the sacraments is guarded by the local church and they are kept together.
Baptism and Eucharist must not be separated from the preaching and
reading of the Word, nor from confession. All work together to bring
glory to God.[14]

RECEIVING TOGETHER

We have hinted at this next section a number of times, but now we want
to say it very clearly: a church is a community. It is not a fluid community
that changes each week like patrons of a local restaurant or the dining
room in a country club. In those places you may have some of the same
people each week, but the community that develops is purely self-serving.
They all pay to be there for their own joy or pleasure. Church is different.
This strange place is shaped and formed solely for others. Everyone
comes to be a servant to others, in service to Jesus Christ. For this reason
many churches have membership. Joining a church is a way of accepting
adoption into this particular family. Church hopping makes faithfulness
and trustworthiness nearly impossible. When we attend a church, we are
merely visitors or entertainment seekers.

When we see the local church as our family—a family we cannot easily
divorce—there is the possibility for real transformation. The Bible calls
it sanctification, or becoming more holy (more like Jesus). Transformation takes time, commitment, and humility.

With a view of the church as my family, I receive the teachings and the
sacraments with this family. We are responsible for each other and
accountable to each other. Paul makes this very clear when he gives
instructions about receiving the Lord's Supper in 1 Corinthians. This first
letter that Paul sent to the Corinthian church shows a lot of division
caused (mostly) by big egos among the leaders. Not much has changed,
really. So Paul, not mincing his words at all, tells them to behave.

Actually, they were not behaving. They were suing each other due to
their desire to control the church. In short, the problem was their arrogance. *Arrogance*, by the way, can be understood as the foundational sin
of all sins, and *humility* is the foundational Christian virtue.

Back to 1 Corinthians and Christian unity. In 1 Corinthians 11 Paul gives instructions about the Lord's Supper (as we looked at above), but first he talks about abuses in worship. There are divisions, false motives, and people who are unrepentant receiving the elements. This type of worship both misrepresents Jesus and causes further division. Thus, as a family, we need to be reconciled before we eat. My father was very strong about this. He loved his family, but he also loved us to get along. If we were arguing at the table, or if we came to dinner angry, he got very stern and warned us. One time (and it only happened once), I complained about the vegetables at dinner and he told me to go down to the basement and "grab my ankles." I never made that mistake again. In fact, we all worked very hard to be unified and reconciled at the table.

The Communion table is a table too. It is not only for eating together, but also for working together, raising our children together, caring for the sick and the aged together. For all of these and many other reasons, we receive the Word and the sacraments as a family, not alone. When, as a family, we hear the reading from the last chapter of Matthew and are confronted with Jesus' last words, we ask, "What about us? What does this mean for our family? How are we, as a family, being faithful to Jesus' command to go to all the nations?" When we hear a Scripture passage that says, "We urge you, brothers and sisters, warn those who are idle and disruptive, encourage the disheartened, help the weak, be patient with everyone" (1 Thess 5:14), we know that this is for us and for our family. We live into this teaching by actually helping the weak and disheartened in our local family.

One final note on receiving as a family: Most of the work of the church, being the body of Christ in our local community, involves doing work together. Long-term faithful service together is a rare thing today, but the world needs it, and we are given this very gift: a real community of people who are committed to me and I to them so we can love others as Jesus has loved us. Mission requires community. (We will look at this more carefully in the following chapter.)

RECEIVING THE WORD AND WATCHING VIDEOS

Imagine this if you will: A little over five hundred years ago there was a new experience in worship and Bible reading. During worship someone was reading from his own Bible in worship. In fact, a few people in the congregation had *their own* copies of the Bible! It was like a miracle, to have your own copy of God's Word. Previously, without moveable type, very few Bibles actually existed. Now people could actually read the Bible silently, to themselves, without making any noise. This was a new experience for the church. It is hard to believe, but as I mentioned in the section on the reading of Scripture, for most of the life of the church, people did not have their own Bibles to read. Now we do, and so we can (so few do, though) read the Bible for hours each week! But our *connection* to that tradition now has a new *context*; we live in a very visual culture. People have a hard time reading long texts of books. They read texts (and tweets), but seldom books. Technology is changing our ways of learning, and even the ways our brain is being shaped.

Early in the present century I was teaching a Christian history class in Sabah, East Malaysia. The students were from about eight ethnic groups and also from four different countries. I opened my Bible to read a passage from Scripture before the history lesson would start. As I pulled out my Bible I noticed that two students pulled out their cell phones. This was my first experience watching people read the Bible from their phones. It would be another ten years before I had a Bible app on my phone! Now we receive daily devotionals from Christian apps on our phones, and we can have sermons downloaded to listen to during our morning commutes to work. We are still connected to the Word, but our context for receiving the Word has become much more complex.

Few new churches are buying hymnals today. Many churches use visual representations for announcements, texts of Scripture, sermon outlines, even pictures and videos to illustrate sermons. It would be unwise to try to reverse technology and science. However, it would also be foolish *not* to think about what this means as a Christian. The purpose of worship as we are describing it in these few chapters is to *live into Jesus Christ*—his life, his sufferings, his joy, his mind, and his mission. We expect to be changed because we are part of a church and because we worship. Entertainment seldom changes people. Entertainment is self-serving and self-affirming, and much technology is dedicated to entertainment. A few questions here may help to evaluate the place of technology in worship:

1. Does our use of technology help people to understand more deeply the meaning of Scripture, the sufferings of Christ, or the glory of his nature?

2. Is our use of technology simply making people more comfortable, or does it also make it easier to understand hard teachings or ideas?

3. Does the use of technology help to make the congregation stronger and more committed to Jesus and his Church?

4. Are the images gratuitous or profound? Are they trite and cute or do they challenge and draw people in to think more deeply about an idea. As a general rule, "less is more."

A little educational theory might help at this point. For people to learn, to deepen their faith and zeal for the Lord, they need to think. Jesus was very good at getting people to think. He seldom said things in a straightforward manner (although he did occasionally), but he told parables, gave illustrations, and asked questions. All of these techniques drive others to think. His teachings were profound and thought provoking. He said things like, "Show me the coin used for paying the tax. . . . Whose image is this?" (Mt 22:18-21). "I am the gate for the sheep" (Jn 10:7). "Anyone who loves their life will lose it, while anyone who hates their life in this world will keep it for eternal life" (Jn 12:25). Wow, these little sentences demand some thought.

The brain is basically lazy, and so it needs to be encouraged to think or else it will just go on automatic pilot. Technology can help people think more deeply about a topic, or it can make it so easy that we not only won't think about a sermon, but the message may just slide right past our soul. Images in worship should be less, not more, and they should provoke thought more than overstate a concept.

RECEIVING AND RETELLING: WORD AND WITNESS

When my wife and I had recently graduated from college, we attended a large conference held between Christmas and New Year's Day. It was just Nancy, me, and an intimate group of 17,000 other college students. The Urbana Missions Conference is a remarkable event that provides up-to-date content on mission work in the world, good biblical teaching about mission, engaging drama, and electrifying worship in song. The prayer that supports the work of the conference is extensive, broad, and continuous (I later learned).

When we attended many years ago, it changed our lives. We heard testimonies of missionaries, we sang songs about God's great love, we saw informative video shows, but what was most engaging for me was hearing the Bible taught by the great Anglican priest and Bible teacher John Stott. His teaching was so memorable and motivational that on the last night of the convention, under the encouragement of Billy Graham, we decided to sign a statement to serve as missionaries overseas. John Stott's teaching (or preaching, I am not sure what it was!) I still remember today. "Our God is a missionary God. The Lord Christ is a missionary Christ. The Holy Spirit is a missionary Spirit." Finally, "The Church is a missionary church!" We were absolutely convinced and convicted.

From preaching the Word, we went out to serve this missionary God. We were not that unusual, really. Not that all 17,000 people went out to be missionaries, but the movement from receiving the Word proclaimed to going out to witness to others—that is the normal Christian life. We receive to share. We are filled with the fullness of Christ in order to be the presence of Christ to the world around us. This is the normal Christian life. It is a wonderful, healthy, fulfilling life, but it is also dangerous and often involves suffering. However, the sufferings are not to be compared with the joy and glory to follow.

Okay, we have been sitting long enough, now let's go! Chapter seven, please.

7

GO

IT IS ALWAYS INTERESTING WHEN I visit a new church to see how they greet us, or if they even notice that we are there. One church we visited I remember very well. We were greeted cordially, someone asked if we live in the area, and then we were given some information about the church, and we were taken to a seat and introduced to someone sitting nearby. Very nice. But what was even more interesting was that during a time to greet others (that very uncomfortable time when you don't know if you should wait for people to come to you, or if you should turn to the right or the left) we were given a card to fill out. The card had a place for name and contact information and then it had three sections: (1) Needs; (2) Ministry; (3) Witness. Each person was encouraged to tell what needs they may have (prayer, healing, a job, housing, etc.). Then they were given a chance to tell how they might serve *inside* the church (singing, finances, children, youth, etc.). Finally, every person was asked how they wanted to be involved in witness *outside* the church. It was assumed that everyone would have needs and would be able to serve in the church and would have a type of witness outside the church.

Church is not a filling station, nor is it a clinic, concert hall, an emergency room, or even a spa. It is not a place we go to get fixed or to be entertained or distracted. Church is not personal therapy as much as it is community, training, and (dare I say it?) warfare.

The local church functions more like an outpost, a signpost, or even a blog post. Existing in enemy territory, the local church is an outpost of divine presence. It is a signpost pointing to the kingdom of God, and it is a blog post of God's Word in the midst of a cacophony of mindless and soulless words. It is important to understand these distinctions or else we might think of church as like the tabernacle or temple in the Old Testament or like Mecca for Muslims: a sacred place where God shows up.

The distinction between sacred places and profane places served an important role in the Old Testament that does not apply for Christians. The Old Testament temple is gone. God now tabernacles (camps) with his people; John 1:14 says that the Word (Jesus) made his dwelling (tabernacle) among us. In 2 Chronicles 29–30, Hezekiah brought about a reform: he opened the doors of the temple, repaired the doors, had the temple cleaned of idols, and then had the people sanctify themselves for sacred worship in this very sacred place. Everyone had to come to that sacred place to worship the one true God. Hezekiah sent out word to Israel, north of Judah, that they should also come to Jerusalem to worship. Even the nations (the non-Jews) would learn about God by coming to Jerusalem. The *place* was sacred. Other places were not.

Ezra and Nehemiah show a similar renewed concern to remake Jerusalem as a sacred place of God's presence for God's people. Rebuilding the wall first was a way of keeping out the unholy nations, nations whose worship was degrading to both deity and humanity. Both Ezra and Nehemiah end in what seems a very callous and strange way: excluding all the foreign women. This view of what is holy and sacred differs greatly from the view for the church.

This idea of sacred and secular or of holy and unholy places changed with the incarnation: God came to earth as a human being. In the incarnation we learn that God has now sanctified humans (not places). In fact, he has sanctified all humans of all races and nations. We, who have the image of God on us, are to be God's temple (1 Cor 3:16-17; 6:18-20; 1 Pet 2:5). We live and move and have our being throughout the earth, and so we bring temple worship (really!) to all places. In this sense—listen carefully—*worship becomes mission.*

We worship in the midst of the nations bringing the good news to every community. The reverse is also true. Mission is worship—that is, honoring Jesus and his kingdom in and among the nations.

So, before talking about "go," we want to eradicate the false dichotomy that has been so prevalent among Christians: the view that mission is a separate activity or part of the church. This is more than a bad representation of mission; it is a dangerous lie.

Mission is the meaning of our worship, and worship is the power and purpose of our mission. An analogy of the body may help. A brain is a physical chunk of very soft and very complex tissue wrapped in a very hard skull. A mind is . . . well, it is a terrible thing to waste, but it is not the brain. However, can someone talk about a mind without having a brain? Can a brain really exist that does not have a mind? Not if it is a living, functioning body. So the church's existence can best be seen as two interwoven and mutually reinforcing purposes: worship and witness. It is all of one fabric, a fabric that declares God's glory.

COME AND GO: CHAPTERS THREE AND SEVEN

In our discussion of "come" in chapter three, "come" represents conversion (among other things). "Come" means come to Jesus or come to the cross. We come by turning away from the false gods of our world and turning to, even absolutely trusting, the one true God. Conversion is a wonderful thing, really.

I have found that I get along pretty well with converts (that is people who converted to Jesus Christ and remember it!). I am a convert myself. My parents did a very good job taking me to the church and showing me the way, but God's Spirit seemed to have covered my eyes and stopped up my ears until the right time. I had no spiritual ears to *hear* that the good news I was hearing was good news *for me*. This is biblical; we read about this phenomenon in a number of places in the Bible. Jesus says that this is why he spoke in parables, so that, "Seeing they will not see and hearing they will not understand" (Lk 8:10). It is confusing, but God is God, and by his grace, at the age of sixteen, God opened my eyes and cleared out my ears. A great transformation took place. It changed my life and had a transformative impact on all those close to me: my basketball team, soccer team, class officers at high school, my parents, and my sisters. I began to think in different ways and do different things and ask different types of questions. My parents were concerned at first because the change was so dramatic. I became an evangelist, which is part of the normal Christian life.

Having this wonderful change take place in my life made me want to tell others. I would go with friends to this very large indoor mall and we would look for bored people and talk to them about Jesus. Most of the people were bored husbands if I remember correctly. Wives were shopping and the husbands were patiently waiting, so they met me, and some met Jesus too. I am not sure how many lives were changed through our cold turkey evangelism, but I do not think our meetings and conversations about God were meaningless. I just could not keep silent about my conversion. You see, it really was a *second birth* for me.

Years later I would be at a *first birth*: our first child. This also changed my life (understatement!) and of course I wanted to tell others. I called my parents, I called my sisters. In every conversation for weeks or months, I would sneak in, "Well, you may not know this, but I became a father just last month." I had a new identity: father. I had pictures, I told stories. New births are not to be kept in the house or in the family. There is something wrong with the new father or mother who doesn't want to tell others about the new birth.

Thanksgiving (the foundation of worship) naturally leads to witness. Our joy drives us to want others to enter into this joy. "I tell you that in the same way there will be more rejoicing in heaven over one sinner who repents than over ninety-nine righteous persons who do not need to repent. . . . There is rejoicing in the presence of the angels of God over one sinner who repents" (Lk 15:7, 10). I love joy. We are made for joy.

WORDS: WITNESS, MISSION, AND EVANGELISM

This chapter could be called "Witness," but that word is a little vague. A lawyer reading a chapter by that title might expect to read about a witness in a courtroom ("Sir, what exactly did you see the night of the accident?"). I am using the word *witness* as a collective noun that includes everything the church is sent out into the world to be and to do. I am using the word *witness*, quite honestly, because it starts with *w* and so is easier to remember with the other *w*: worship. Christian witness simply means that the church, and everyone in the church, is called by God and sent by God. Being a Christian is a two-stroke engine, not a stationary statue, more like an ambassador than an idol, more like a courier than a receptionist. We go in to worship, out to witness. In to worship, out to witness.

A normal and healthy Christian life is fed or equipped through worship (come, stand, kneel, sit) so that one can participate in effective witness (go). The Christian life has been described as a pond. A stagnant pond may take in some water upstream, but then it does not allow the water to flow out. It does not flow, recirculate, or even aerate. Stagnant ponds, frankly, smell and are not attractive. They can be deadly. A healthy pond, on the other hand, has water flowing in and also water flowing out. A healthy pond circulates, flows, and aerates. A healthy Christian or a healthy church takes in (chaps. 3, 4, and 6) but does not keep it all in. The health of a church and of a Christian depends on giving away our faith to others.

Witness means testimony. At the ripe old age of twenty-two years and one month, I began my teaching career. I had the good fortune of being prepared well both through my education at a great university and from a wonderful InterVarsity Fellowship group on campus. Our campus group started at about forty people my freshman year. I know this because I counted all the people in that first meeting. It was great! At a secular state university, there were forty Christians gathered to pray, sing, learn, and go out to witness on the campus. We did witness, and four years later there were four hundred in our fellowship group. I learned that this is what you do if you are on a college campus. It seemed like a very normal Christian lifestyle. But I also learned this is the way you should live when you get a job (and my parents were thankful that I did get a job). Find Christians to pray with, study the Bible, and then find ways to witness in your neighborhood and at your place of work. My place of work was a junior high school.

With the (slowly given) permission of the principal, I started a Bible club at this junior high school. I met weekly on Tuesdays after school for about five months with twelve-, thirteen-, and fourteen-year-olds: my disciples. How did I start? I gave my testimony, and my testimony connected us and built trust among us. My testimony was that I had attended church when I was young, but not until I was sixteen did I really hear plainly explained to me that Jesus came for a reason. In a friend's living room one Sunday afternoon in the fall of my junior year a guest said simply, "Jesus' life presents a question for all of us. Do you know what that question is?" I had no idea, but I was very interested. "His life simply says to us, 'Will you follow me or not?'" I had read enough of the Gospels during the first months of our meetings that I knew this sounded true. Jesus was inviting people to follow him. I just had not made the connection that the risen Christ continues to ask that question through his followers. So I answered the question Jesus poses to each person: "Yes, I will follow you, Jesus."

And so I told these twelve young people what happened to me: how I went home, confessed that I needed Jesus, that I could not do it on my own (chaps. 3 and 6), and offered Jesus my life. I told them how I began to read the Bible and how God spoke to me through Scriptures (Lk 9:62). I had put my hand to the plow and here were my instructions from Jesus: Don't look back. Don't second guess. Keep your hand in Jesus' hand.

This is what I told my twelve disciples at the junior high school. When we started meeting, two or three were Christians, but the rest did not attend church at all and had parents who were not going to tell them about Jesus. A testimony, as we noted earlier, is not the gospel, but it is a signpost or illustration of the gospel. If God can save and redirect the life of a self-absorbed sixteen-year-old, or an alcoholic, or a murderer, he can save me. Testimony points to the God of grace and healing. There is no boasting in a testimony; it is all thanksgiving for grace.

Mission means sent. Christians may not realize this, but not all religions are evangelistic. In fact, most religions do not assume that they are to enlist others in their practices or beliefs. Most religions in the history of human existence are ethnic (or cultic) deities: gods that serve their culture or nation. *Lug* for the Celts, *Athena* for the Athenians, *Nyami* for the Akan, or *Ngai* for the Maasai. These religions are not evangelistic.

They are cultural cores, and so we talk about their "cultic"[1] (religious) practices. Hinduism in India is not evangelistic nor is Shintoism in Japan. Judaism was not evangelistic per se, but the expectations were that the Jewish worship would bring others to worship. The queen of Sheba is one of the great and only examples of Jewish witness (1 Kings 10). Judaism says, "Come." Jesus says, "Go."

Jesus made it clear that he represented the only God in the universe and so all that he said and did had relevance for every culture, every people group, every village and city in the world. His was an open secret for all of humanity. His message had universal relevance for every particular people. The universal is included in the particular person of Jesus Christ. When we come to Jesus, we are coming to the missionary of God. But when we come to Jesus, we are not just invited to follow a person; we are invited into the very life of Jesus. A Christian is someone who is "in Christ." In baptism, we are brought into the life of the great missionary of God: Jesus Christ. All those who are called to Jesus are sent by Jesus. Mission means sent.

We are talking about the church in this book, but we have only talked briefly about the establishment of the Church (chap. 2). As a reminder, Jesus established the Church as a sent body, not as a static institution. I have often wondered about other ways Jesus could have established the church: "Now you disciples, stay together and build a new Jesus temple." Or he could have said, "Don't go anywhere, but make sure you organize yourselves well with officers and a reasonable budget." Nothing at all like this happened. Jesus started the church more through sending than establishing, more as a movement than an institution.

John 20:21 says, "As the Father has sent me, I am sending you." Jesus did not say, "As I gathered a group together, so you gather a group together." His final words spoke of going. This was so very different from God's command to Moses, the patriarchs, kings, and prophets. They were to establish a cultural religion: a local religion for their people. Jesus established a movement, an outward movement. The church faces out.

Whether it is from the description in Mathew, Mark, Luke, John, or Jesus' final words before his ascension in Acts (Mt 28:18-20; Mk 16:15-16;

Lk 24:45-49; Jn 20:21-23; Acts 1:8), *the final command from the Lord of the universe is to make disciples by going*. In Matthew, John, and Acts (Acts 1:8 with Acts 2) the commission comes in the midst of worship. It starts with "when they saw him they worshiped him," and then Jesus gives his final instructions that involve going to all the nations of the world. It is a massive, overwhelming responsibility for this small band of frightened Jews. It was a ridiculous command when you think about it. This is the Church at its earliest. Weak and marginalized, but empowered by the risen Christ, they took him at this word and (with some persecution to prod them) they scattered, healed, and proclaimed in the name of Jesus. Church (as well as mission) means *sent*.

Evangelism means announcing good news. What makes good news good is that it is news (and it is about something good). It is information or a report announced to people who have not heard the message before, or who have not had it explained to them. For Christians, who have heard the news and accepted it and can explain it, this good news is no longer *news*. It becomes the good life. No longer is it new; it has become their life, and it is a joyful life. For good news to remain news, it must be told to people who are not in the church, in short, to people who are not family, so that they can become family and can then also have the good life.

Words are very important. In fact, words can kill a person, or words can give life to a person.

Don't we all know people (perhaps you are one) who are just beaten down by the words of others? It is especially painful if the words come from a parent, close friend, or spouse. In these cases the relationship has a level of intimacy and trust, and that is what makes the words especially injurious. Many people are told, "You can't match up," or "You are always making life hard for others," or "It would be better if you just had never been born." We can see that words are not only important, they are also powerful. I have heard such words quite a lot, and at times I speak up; too often I just ignore it. When coaching basketball or soccer I would often hear parents say things like, "Why can't you be a good soccer player like your sister!" I had a friend whose wife was unfaithful to him.

She wanted to get rid of her lawfully wedded husband, so she would say terrible things to him. She would even suggest how he could kill himself. These were just words. But these words eventually did their work and killed someone. Words are powerful.

But words can also give life. A young child who grows up hearing how much they are loved and who sees Dad and Mom show up for the little league game or the school concert is enlivened and empowered. So very many messages tell us we are inadequate, but then God says, "Oh, how much, how very, very much I love you!" He says it, shows it, and says it again. This is very good news, especially since we are living in an age of self-gratification and self-affirmation. All the self stuff becomes nothing more than self-worship, and this brings death to us and our neighbors. But being told unconditionally that we are loved by another restores us and empowers us to love others. Words can give life again and again.

Since words are so powerful and since words can give life, we should use them the way they were made to be used. That is right. Words and the Word made flesh come to give life and joy. The best, most precious and powerful words tell about history: they tell about the birth, life, teachings, death, resurrection, and ascension of Jesus Christ. No other words can compare to these words. Christian witness is much more than words, but it is never less. The words interpret the work of the church in the world.

Many years ago our family sponsored a Vietnamese refugee family. A widow and four children lived in our small apartment just eight months after we had our first child. It was a hard time, but it seemed to be the type of thing a Jesus follower would do, so we and our Bible study group from our local church collected clothes, signed up people for English lessons, took the family shopping, and so many other things. It was a very tiring and difficult time in our lives (I had no idea fish oil could smell up a whole house), but also a very meaningful time. Years later, after they moved to California and we moved to Singapore, we (now with four children) went to visit the family. The mother honored us with gifts and a cake that said, "Thank You Scott and Nancy:

Our Sponsors." It then hit me that for a refugee, a sponsor is like a savior. Without a sponsor you are doomed to a refugee camp or to continued oppression or persecution.

The mother was cutting the cake and then said in Vietnamese something to her daughter. Then the daughter turned to Nancy and me and said very directly: "Why did you do it?" It sounded more like an accusation, but it was an honest query. "Why did we do what?" I asked, thinking I may have spilled something on the carpet. "Why did you sponsor us?" There it was. Coming from a Chinese-Vietnamese culture, such behavior, "laying down your life for your friends," was inexplicable. So I gave the refugee family my testimony. And my testimony, like all testimonies, pointed to Jesus, who changed my life and gave me a new purpose, in fact, a new reason for living. Evangelism announces and explains good news, good news rooted in the life and message of Jesus Christ.

Evangelism also means* being *good news. I almost didn't have this section when I wrote my first draft of this chapter. I wanted the previous section to simply say: "Evangelism means being and announcing good news." However, because so many Christians today have come to believe the cultural lie that telling people about Jesus is offensive, I felt we needed a separate section on evangelistic witness. We need to recover the joy of telling others about Jesus in holy conversations.[2] However, proclaiming good news without demonstrating good news is equally tragic. We illustrate the good news that we tell others about through the good news that we do as a community. Thus, the gospel is revealed in Jesus-like works we do. The love from the One who is love is poured into our lives and overflows into the lives of those around us. It should be a very natural result or outpouring from our own redemption. We receive the healing and reconciliation from God, and we just can't wait to show the same grace and love to others.

I remember so clearly when I came to faith in Christ at the age of sixteen: I immediately wanted to tell my sister, my friends on the soccer team, and my friends in my classes in high school. Many came to faith in Christ, but we, as a small high school fellowship group, also wanted to show God's love to others. And so we did some looking around and we asked adults who knew more about these things. After a year, I was senior class president and decided to use my presidential powers to bless low-income families in a local suburb of Philadelphia. We planned a Thanksgiving party for about twenty families. The senior class officers and others in the senior class got the names from the social services in the town. In an age less concerned about legal issues, we picked up the families in our own cars, brought them to the high school, and fed them a great Thanksgiving dinner. After the dinner we gave out gifts and took time to sing Christmas carols. It is hard to believe, but we actually cooked the turkeys ourselves in the school kitchen and set the tables and served about one hundred people. I am sure there were other ways we could have shown the love of God, but for seventeen-year-old high school students, it was a good start to our Christian lives. Not all of the students were committed Christians at the start and not all of the families were active Christians, but by the end, most of us were on a path drawing us much closer to Jesus. As I think back about it today, it really was a miraculous time, but it was also a natural response to our own conversion. We were becoming good news for others.

One final word about evangelism in word and life: in a very self-inflated world, it is important that the message we give is not *our* message, but is *God's* message. We can make sure this is true in a number of ways, but the best way (as I have mentioned earlier) is to memorize large portions of the Bible.

Start here with Bible memorization: one passage a month

Psalm 23	Luke 6:27-36
Psalm 67	Luke 10:1-9
Psalm 42	John 15:1-16 (or John 17:1-26)
Psalm 46	
Matthew 5:1-16	Philippians 4:4-9
Matthew 11:28-30	(or Philippians 2:1-11)
Matthew 28:16-20	Revelation 7:9-17

Then, when we speak we can pray for God's Word to be enlivened in our words. Again and again I have seen this happen. The few passages that I have memorized have been used in general conversations, in sermons, and especially in evangelistic conversations. There is no need to talk about a specific view of inspiration of the Bible. We simply need to acknowledge what Christians around the world and throughout history have affirmed: "The word of God is alive and active. Sharper than any double-edged sword, it penetrates even to dividing soul and spirit, joints and marrow; it judges the thoughts and attitudes of the heart" (Heb 4:12). If this is true—and it is—we should have as much of the Word of God in our heart as possible.

GOING OUT AS CROSSING BOUNDARIES

Full disclosure: the idea for this book in your hands came from one small section of a book I published five years ago, entitled *Understanding Christian Mission: Participation in Suffering and Glory.*[3] That book had a section on the Church to explain that God's mission is to be carried out from the church into the world. In that book I first used the concept of body movements (come, stand, kneel, sit, go) to explain what church is all about. It was just impossible to talk about mission without talking about church. But it is also impossible (or at least inaccurate) to talk about the church and to ignore the place of mission or witness in the life of the local church and the Church universal. Mission flows from the Church, and the Church exists for mission.

To risk being too repetitive, the Church has only two purposes, not three or four or more—an idea we talked about in the introduction. Now it is time to refresh our memories. We could do this by looking again at the inauguration of the Church in Matthew 28:16-20, but I also find it helpful to look at that church as it lived into Jesus' commission.

In Acts 2 we read about the coming of the Holy Spirit with such power that onlookers raised questions. It was no secret that they were worshiping the formerly dead (now very alive and active) Jesus from Nazareth. I often pray for such power in worship, such power that others ask, "What in the world is going on here?" In Acts 2, questions were asked and, when others were paying attention, Peter preached a powerful sermon about Jesus. Such a sermon brought about the salvation of 3,000 people. They continued to be faithful to Jesus and his teaching, "breaking bread," praising God, and as a result, "the Lord added to their number daily those who were being saved" (Acts 2:47). Worship overflowed to witness. Witness led to more in worship. It was the natural life of the church that was inaugurated with a commission.

That very earliest church did not remain a cultural or a local church. Immediately people from many languages and cultures were involved. We might say that two boundaries were crossed by the earliest church as recorded in Acts. If these two boundaries were not crossed, I would not be writing this book today because the Jesus movement would have remained as a Jewish sect.

The first boundary that was crossed was the boundary of language and geography. We see this in that earliest worship on the day of Pentecost. People were in Jerusalem from Parthia (today in Iran or Iraq), Turkey, Syria, Egypt, Crete, North Africa, and Arabia. These people spoke both trade languages (Greek, Syriac, Aramaic, and probably Latin) as well as local languages. They were a multicultural group of Jewish worshipers. Some were involved in trade, and many had been refugees forced off their land by the conquest of Babylon, centuries earlier. Now they came to worship at the temple in Jerusalem and they each heard in their own language, in their mother tongue (not the trade language), the good news about Jesus the Messiah. This miraculous translation of the gospel into the heart language of foreigners is the first boundary to be crossed.

The idea of translation did not start with John Wycliffe, or with the Reformation, but with God's Holy Spirit in Acts 2.

> The gospel is meant to be translated for all to hear.

Thus, we have a very strong hint of the importance of crossing this boundary with all people. No one should be excluded from hearing the greatest story ever told. In fact, it is the obligation of the Church to reduce the barriers that would make it difficult to "hear" Jesus speak. On a recent trip to China, I saw this concern to

cross language barriers clearly displayed. At a special anniversary celebration of a seminary in China, my speech was translated sentence by
sentence into Mandarin. At the same time, about forty delegates who
were hearing impaired had the message translated into sign language
while someone typed the message into Chinese characters onto a Power-
Point slide. Each sentence delivered into four languages to make sure
everyone could hear in their own language.[4] I immediately thought
about how my own local church makes it easy for everyone to hear or
how we exclude people through language.

But the gospel also crossed a second barrier in Acts, one that opened
up the gospel to all the people and people groups in the world. Acts 10–15
tells the full story of this difficult transition. Before Acts 10, it seemed to
be the assumption of the early Jewish Christians that a person still must
be a religious Jew to come to faith in Jesus: from idol worshiper to Jewish
God-fearer to Christian. If Jesus came to complete the Law, then we still
in some way must be under the Law first. A miracle was needed to break
the early Christians out of this idea of Jewish priority in salvation. In
fact, two miracles, no, actually *three* miracles were needed. The first
miracle was that a gentile Roman soldier who was a God-fearer,
Cornelius, had a vision. A large and powerful angel appeared to him and
frightened him and told him that his prayers were answered and he
should send for Peter to explain things to him. This was the first miracle.

The second miracle was that Peter, a devout Jew and humbled follower
of Jesus, twenty-one hours later was sitting on a rooftop, "fell into a
trance" (Acts 10:10), had a vision, and heard a voice that basically said the
dietary restrictions from the Old Testament Law no longer applied. He
could now eat whatever he wanted (even shellfish and reptiles!). Peter
could eat bacon and still be holy before God. Immediately after he had
this vision, the emissaries of Cornelius arrived inviting Peter to come to
Caesarea. This was the second miracle.

The third was a miracle for Peter (and the Jesus-following Jews) and
Cornelius (and the God-fearing Gentiles) together. While Peter was
doing his job of explaining about Jesus, the Holy Spirit came upon all
who heard the word (the uncircumcised Gentiles), and they began

praising God, speaking in tongues. It was like the experience Peter had in Acts 2: while he was preaching, the Holy Spirit came upon others in an audible and undeniable way. All nations were to receive the teachings of Jesus directly, without having to become religious or even cultural Jews. Three miracles were needed to show that all nations, all religions, all cultures can receive Jesus. In fact, it is the Church's obligation to make sure they all do hear.

To frame it differently, it is God's joyous enterprise to bring the good news to every group of people in the world in their own culture and language. It is the joy of the church to be the body of Christ to fulfill this enterprise. All

> Redemption is accomplished in Christ, through cultures and families.

churches and each local church share in this life for the redemption of the world.

Local churches find their full life as they embrace this purpose that is beyond themselves and even beyond their local communities. In Christian witness we are called to move out of our Christian community, out of our local parish or church neighborhood into the broader world. This movement out involves crossing boundaries, moving across barriers of class, race, language, and nation. To put it bluntly: a static or stationary church is a contradiction.

Inclusive mission, extensive going. We can talk about this global dimension of the local church's missional obligation in many ways, but one way tells how God's mission is inclusive and extensive. It is to the end of the earth ("all nations," Mt 28:19) and to the end of time (Mt 28:20). The Church must seek to *include* all people (in their own cultures) and it is to *extend* to every dimension of a life and a culture. Many, many mission organizations and many plans for evangelizing the world exist today. Some organizations and plans are more biblical and Christlike than others, but none is perfect. However, every local congregation does not have the luxury of staying aloof of plans and organizations that seek to reach the unreached and love the unloved in the world. Every local congregation and every local Christian has accepted the mission of God to the nations when receiving into our lives the Lord of the nations. If we do not join with other movements and organizations, we will have to create our own.

Accept Jesus; accept his mission. Assuming that most of the people reading this book are in the West, or the affluent non-Western world, it could be argued that we are even more obligated to be actively involved in global mission. Compared to the global population, 88 percent of US citizens are upper or high upper class. We may not feel it, but we are wealthy, and this should give us pause. Jesus talked about the wealthy using pretty strong words: "It is easier for a camel to go through the eye of a needle than for someone who is rich to enter the kingdom of heaven" (Mt 19:24). We who are rich by global standards have an obligation to stop investing in ourselves and in material goods and instead invest in things eternal: "But store up for yourselves treasures in heaven, where moths and vermin do not destroy, and where thieves do not break in and steal" (Mt 6:20). I believe investing in heaven means investing in the lives of people so that others can hear the good news of Jesus and experience his love and healing power. Such investment not only demonstrates obedience, it is also good for our own souls. Unfortunately our souls are very sick. Instead of investing radically (even recklessly) in heaven, we rich Christians in the West spend most of our money on ourselves. This is a moral and spiritual dilemma.

Western Christians do give to missionary work, but most of the money that we give goes to the already evangelized. Only 0.1 percent (that is, a tenth of one percent) of Christian giving goes to the thirty-eight least-evangelized countries in the world.[5] We can argue about the precision of this statistic, but even if it is only vaguely close to accurate, it is a tremendous injustice. Why should the richest people in the world spend so much on themselves and continue to ignore the people most estranged from the Savior of the world? We spend 95 percent of our offerings on ourselves, on our home ministries, which means on our local churches.

When we talk about the final body movement of the church, "go," it absolutely, positively, and categorically means go to every nation and every ethnic group of people. No dichotomy exists between going across the street and going across the oceans. However the needs (medical, evangelistic, nutritional, etc.) are far, far greater outside of the West. Each church should evaluate its love of the Savior and his mission by looking at its budget and checkbook. Then the church leaders can ask, "How are we using our human resources? Does our use of time and our use of money reflect the heart and mind of Jesus, whom we now live with and in?"

Many years ago I attended a church that was desperate for a pastor. I was just in high school, but I remember even today the divisiveness of the congregation. The two major factions agreed on a pastoral candidate, but when the candidate looked at the church budget, he gave them an ultimatum. "I will come to be your pastor if you begin to change your priorities. If you increase your mission giving 5 percent a year until it reaches 50 percent of the church income, then I will come. Without this commitment I will not come." Well, he came, and the church was transformed. As more and more money was being given to mission, the church leaders had to find more and more ways to give to others. Houses were built for the poor in the region. Churches were built overseas. Members of the congregation were sent out as missionaries and supported by the church. We were one of the families sent out and strongly supported by this congregation. Why shouldn't every church give 50 percent of its money to mission outside of its four walls? Why not 60 percent?

Every local congregation should be a community connected to far-off places where people need the knowledge and the love of Jesus Christ. No dichotomies: every type of mission work engages in loving acts and loving words as one action. Praying for starving people while trying to feed the most malnourished is not being superspiritual—it is being consistent. By God's Holy Spirit, the missionary brings something of the presence of Jesus even when there is little she or he can do to alleviate suffering.

The following psalm expresses it well. When we look into the face of Jesus, we turn then to make God's Word and ways known to all the nations of the world. The goal seeks for all the nations to praise God, for all the nations to be filled with joy. We look forward to the land providing food for all (to meet the needs of all people) and for all people (to the ends of the earth) to fear God.

> May God be gracious to us and bless us,
>   and make his face to shine upon us—
> so that your ways may be known on earth,
>   your salvation among all nations.
>
> May the peoples praise you, God;
>   may all the peoples praise you.
> May the nations be glad and sing for joy,
>   for you rule the peoples with equity
>   and guide the nations of the earth.
> May the peoples praise you, God;
>   may all the peoples praise you.
>
> The land yields its harvest;
>   God, our God, blesses us.
> May God bless us still,
>   so that all the ends of the earth will fear him. (Ps 67)

CHURCH AS MISSIONAL PRESENCE

It is true that mission *beyond* our community and beyond our borders is the calling of every church. But it is also true that "go!" means we go out from the Christian community (church) to be the good news for others *in* our community. The way we see our families, our communities, our schools, our places of work, and our world makes us that good news. Churches become the good news for their communities in the way they see their communities with the eyes of Jesus and the way their hearts are broken with the things that break the heart of Christ. Let me give a few examples of how local churches today might see their own communities and our own culture with the eyes of Jesus. When Jesus sees families today, does he see reconciled couples supporting each other and (together) guiding their children to godliness? Or does he see the rising rates of divorce, family violence, and births out of wedlock as special concerns of his love? I believe Jesus not only sees the need for peace and reconciliation in families in the West today, but he also weeps over the pain of alienation, violence, and woundedness. Scripture considers all families important, yet today local churches are confronted with such brokenness and pain it is hard to know where to begin being the love of God for our church members even before we move outside the church.

And how does Jesus see the growing problem of homelessness (generally compounded by the complex issues of mental illness, addiction, unemployment, and affordable housing)? How does Jesus see racial injustices and violence across ethnic and racial lines? The compassion of Christ should open our eyes to those around us. Jesus walked along the road and *heard* the blind beggar, he *saw* Zacchaeus in the tree, and he *felt* the touch of the bleeding woman. His attentiveness—listening, looking, and feeling—to the needs around him shows how we should grow in our own awareness of the needs for healing, reconciliation, and compassion. In each of our own churches we will have to discuss and study the best ways to bring healing and reconciliation to such complex issues as homelessness, mental illness, and affordable medical care. But as a local church we should be involved in these discussions, always working toward being the presence of Christ in our community and for those in need. This is the good news of Christ lived for our neighbor.

Lesslie Newbigin, a pastor and missionary, is reported to have made the interesting observation about the local church in a local community. He said that the local church should become so valuable to the local community in its care for the poor, support for children and the elderly, that if the local governing authorities wanted to tear down the church to build a shopping mall, all the local citizens would protest. Not just the Christians, but all the local people would realize the value of the church, its life for the community, and would rise up to defend the importance of the church for their community. I think this is true.

A local church's presence should be value added for all those around. More churches should mean more human thriving as more and more people experience the loving presence of Christ. The righteous will rejoice, and only the wicked need be concerned.[6]

Missional. In 1998 a new word was defined: missional.[7] Despite a long tradition of Christians talking about the missionary nature of the Christian life and of the local church, now Christians began using the word *mission* as an adjective: *missional*. This added a new way to describe this purpose of the church. Now that we have this helpful adjective, what does it mean? It means many things today, but I would like to return to its initial, twentieth-century meaning. In its original usage, *missional* derives from the nature of God, who is a sending or missionary God. Since God by his very nature is a missionary God, we who are made in his image and who participate in the life of his Son are missionary in our very being. What does this mean? And what does this say about the church?

In brief, this means that the church in any local context should be understood as sent *to that context*. A church does not just happen to have property, or a building, or a house in which to gather together. It may look that way to the initiated, but every local church is a body of Christians who were sent to that particular community. This means that when we pray in our churches, we pray for our community; we were sent to this place! When we walk out of our building after worship, we remember that we are walking into our life as missionaries of the living God.

What does *missional* mean for the elementary school teacher? It means that she understands her calling to bring the presence of Christ into the school and the classroom. She does not leave Jesus out in the parking lot; he enters with the teacher and with the Christian students. Every classroom, every gym class, and every choir rehearsal is a place of Christian presence and practice. The teacher should bathe her students, the staff, and the other faculty with prayer. What does missional mean for the businessperson, the college student, or the barista at a coffee shop? It means the same thing. Both corporately and individually, the local church sends out its people to be the presence of Christ in the coffee shop, in the dormitory, or at the office. On one level we can say that every Christian is sent out as a local missionary. Part of that mission is to pray for the hurting,

> *Missional* means that each individual realizes, I am sent to my community, school, and place of work.

listen to the lonely, announce to the ignorant, and invite all to become part of the kingdom.

Corporately, *missional* means that the local church is attentive to the needs of the local community and to opportunities to proclaim the joyous news to various groups and contexts in its local community. When we become aware of drug trafficking and gang violence, the local church responds. A missional response requires listening to local community leaders before deciding to do something. It also requires a biblically Christian analysis that looks below the surface of violence or addictions to the root causes found in broken relationships, injustices, and ignorance. Local churches cannot solve all the problems of a city or a town, but they can and should be counted on as first responders and reliable partners in both announcing and displaying the kingdom to those around. Missional existence is really nothing that special. It is Christian existence, the basic Christian lifestyle.

Lifestyle that connects. When we served as missionaries in Asia, we returned on furlough one summer, and I went out to breakfast with my pastor (the pastor who challenged the church to increase mission giving each year). Although he was very supportive of us, I did not know him very well because he had come to my home church after I had gone off to college. I learned a great deal from him that one morning that we got together to talk. We went to a local restaurant, and as we entered he greeted the hostess and asked about her family. Then we went in the kitchen, unannounced (really), he just barged in and talked to the chef. Next he found another waiter and talked to him about how his mother was doing. Finally, he found the manager and asked if he wanted to join us at church on Sunday to hear a missionary speak (me). The restaurant was his parish and he seemed responsible for these people even though only one person in the restaurant attended his church. I have no idea what we talked about that morning. I had my heart and mind changed about the church before we ordered coffee—and that is all I remember.

One of my favorite book titles is Rebecca Manley Pippert's *Out of the Salt Shaker and Into the World*.[8] It is a wonderful book about making sure that Christians, in this case Christians in colleges and universities, do not stay with Christians all the time. Jesus made it very clear that we are to be a lamp on a lamp stand, a city on a hill, and we are not to lose our saltiness. This means that we are saved to be in the world, as Jesus was in the world. If we come to faith in Jesus Christ and only remain close to other Christians, then the very reason for our existence in this world is negated. We are of no value to the world if we neglect our joyous task of engaging the hurts and ignorance of those around us. Rather, we are blessed to be a blessing; healed to be healers; loved to love others. A healthy church that comes, stands, kneels, and sits will send out people who add salt to the world.

ONE BODY AND ONE MISSION

Mission by myself or with my church has its problems, but they are small problems. Working with others is a big problem. It seems that one of Jesus' greatest concerns before he was crucified was that his followers would stay united to him *and* to each other. Jesus' prayer in John 17 displays a clear connection between our unity and witness to others. Our witness pointing to Jesus as the Messiah, the Lord of the nations, will be clear and believable if we remain united. Our divisions make our words less believable. Think about it. How can we talk about God's grace and love for all when we cannot get along with other believers? It is critical that we confess our divisions and pray for greater unity among Christians (even those who we suspect are too liberal or conservative, or patriotic, or unpatriotic, etc.). This is mandatory for the health of our congregations and the credibility of our witness.

We can think about this in many ways. Let me suggest one way: make "unity in mission" or "partnership in mission" your watchword. In other words, don't let people in your congregation talk about or participate in mission without using the language and the practice of bringing others along in mission with you. No church should do local, regional, or global outreach alone. Here are some simple examples.

If your church is an urban church with concerns about gangs, homelessness, and families, then walk through the neighborhoods and find all the local churches or gatherings of Jesus' followers and start to pray together. No rush. Pray together for a year. Have all-night prayer meetings for the neighborhoods, the schools, the streets, and the families. Wait on the Lord as you pray and study the Bible together. Then when you begin to act, you act as one community of believers from various churches in the city.

If you are a church in a small town, start with the same concern: unity in mission. Plan some gatherings with local church leaders to study some of the local issues (drug trafficking, literacy, unemployment, etc.) together and to pray. Again, don't rush this. Take time to build trust and become friends in Jesus Christ who is the missionary of God. This Jesus will then lead you together into his mission for the neighborhood.

The same basic approach can be used for regional and global mission. Don't launch out alone, but find some local churches to cooperate with. This can be done for mission trips, bringing together black churches, Korean churches, Hispanic churches along with multicultural and mostly white churches to go on mission trips together, or to send out missionary families together. However you work it out, you have the constant refrain "unity in mission" calling you forward. God's mission is not a corporate or private enterprise. It is a public, intercultural, local, and global movement of the people of God working together to see his glory revealed among the nations. It is a beautiful thing as we see unlikely companions participating in God's wonderful joy for the world.

MISSION IS NOT AN ELECTIVE

Some people sing in the choir, some teach the Bible, and some people "do missions." Well, actually, it is true that many of us should not sing in a choir, but participation in God's mission is not an elective, it is a core curriculum course. All who are called to Christ are sent by Christ. Can a person come to faith, start attending a local church, and not tell others about Jesus? Well, I guess they can, but if they are mute in their witness they have not yet understood what it means to be a Christian. There is a direct connection between believing in Jesus and speaking to others about Jesus. As Paul puts it, "'I believed, and so I spoke'—we also believe, and so we speak" (2 Cor 4:13 NRSV). Christians cannot opt out of mission—not if they understand even a small piece of how great God's love is for them.

Churches are not fortresses, nor are they monasteries or merely sanctuaries. They should function as a safe place or sanctuary for those whose lives are exposed and damaged. But churches are not only sanctuaries. Churches are places of gathered worship, public witness, and launching stations. All the above. A recent book title grabbed my attention, *Breaking the Huddle: How Your Community Can Grow Its Witness.*[9] What a great image! The global church and each local gathering must break their huddle and head out to the places of pain, loss, and alienation in the world. If you can remember back to the second paragraph of this chapter, the church is an outpost, a signpost, and even a blog post for the world.

The church, we now see, is God's plan for the whole earth: to the ends of the earth. It is God's only plan. God did not say that seminaries or NGOs or wealthy foundations would bring the kingdom of God. The Church is God's plan A as well as his plan B. Don't ever expect God to say, "Oh, no. The Church is really messing it up. I had no idea this would happen! I am going to work through big and wealthy foundations now." It is the Church alone.

Christian mission is the overflow of praise, the excess of love that God pours into our wounded souls and that seeps into the lives of our neighbors and our not-yet neighbors.

Go.

> *Enter to Celebrate*
> *Depart to Proclaim*[10]

8

HEALTHY BODY MOVEMENT

NANCY AND I STILL HAVE A VERY STRONG positive memory of entering the Virginia Beach Community Chapel for worship on Sunday mornings and seeing on the wall, spread over about thirty or forty feet, a massive and beautifully carved map of the world. Above the wood-carved image was the simple phrase and reminder for those worshiping, "All the World Is on God's Heart." It was impossible to enter a worship service, centered as it was on biblical preaching, and not think about the rest of the world. Worship and witness were interwoven every Sunday, and throughout the week.

The church has only two purposes: worship and witness. This volume seems to have focused more on worship, but that is because healthy and vital worship is so important for mission to be effective. Worship fuels mission. Worship humanizes us. Worship empowers us for mission. Worship overflows into witness. Witness that does not flow out of vital, re-centering, and empowering worship is not worthy to be called Christian mission. A healthy church pays attention to all five movements, but there is more.

Who in the world, when they have experienced something as remarkable and beautiful as the birth of their first child, cannot witness to others what has happened? We just cannot keep silent. "Since Christ is Lord of heav'n and earth, how can I keep from singing?"[1] I remember very well trying to get to a phone to call my parents when each one of our children was born. I also remember getting those phone calls from our children when their children were born. The joy of life, new life, or the life of vital worship, like a lake after a storm, overflows the dam. The love of God overflows into the world as love for neighbor.

In this final chapter I want to put together the previous movements and lift up some issues that have returned again and again in the past. Many of these issues have less to do with facts and more to do with feelings and relationships. I will talk about joy, lament, personal relationships, and identity. These issues play a part in every church, but we seldom talk about them. After you read this chapter, you can talk about them with your church.

ORDER AND ARDOR

This volume discusses the five basic body movements chronologically, as though every church should order their life and their worship this way. Of course, this order is reasonable and it makes good biblical and theological sense. We do have to first convert, or turn to the cross before we worship or praise God, and we do need to know who God is before we are led to confession and repentance. And, in general it is good to make sure your mission or Christian witness springs up from vital worship. (Please, make sure that you pray before you witness!) These body movements serve as good reminders for Christians and especially for Christian leaders. However, the basic body movements should not be a straightjacket; there are times when this order is just not possible or helpful. Sometimes praise just does not end, or the purpose of the gathering is only praise. At other times Bible study is the purpose of the gathering and there is just not time (or it is not appropriate) to have a period of confession.

Thus, order serves us well in reminding us of the basic areas of church life and the purpose of our life in community. I have offered these five body movements as a way to prevent oversimplification of the church or reductionism in worship or church life.

Sometimes you hear a lesson or read a book and remember very well what it was about. I remember from many years ago reading a book by an important church leader of the middle of the twentieth century: John A. Mackay. A Scotsman, Mackay was a missionary to Latin American universities before he headed up the Presbyterian mission agency in New York and then became the president of Princeton Theological Seminary. In all of these exalted positions, he remained a devout Christian and missionary at heart. In 1953 he wrote a significant book on Ephesians called *God's Order: The Ephesian Letter and This Present Time*.[2] Mackay's wonderful reminder, even coming from a rather formal Presbyterian, was that the church requires order, but must not lose its ardor. *Ardor* is a word we do not use much in the twenty-first century, but it is a good word. Synonyms for ardor include fervor, zeal, fire, intensity, emotion, gusto, passion, or enthusiasm.

At times a local church or a denomination or network of churches becomes so reasonable and rational that if the Holy Spirit wanted to bring a great emotional revival, he would be turned out. We can be so "ordered" that we lose our attentiveness to spiritual zeal and fire. I am thankful that when I was a young Christian of sixteen and seventeen years old that the leaders in our church gave us room for expressing emotional joy and excitement, even though we often "got it wrong" in the worship services that we ran on our own. We were so excited about knowing Jesus that we started our own worship service in the evening for the community, and we decided to run our own spring retreat in the mountains. They gave us room for our very disordered zeal for the Lord. Because of that room, most of us are still strong Christians today. A healthy church should expect deeply emotional times of worship and mission. We should remember that revival often is not well ordered and rational.

COMMUNITY OF WORSHIP AND WITNESS

The global church and each local church today must address two major theological concerns, which can be expressed as questions:

1. What is the church?

2. Who is Jesus?

Nearly all of our divisions over worship style or interpretation of the Bible and how to live have at their root these two questions. I see so much confusion today about what the church is that I was motivated to write a book about it. You are almost done reading it. I believe that a healthy understanding of the church will bring about greater unity (something Jesus deeply desires) and greater cultural influence (the second great purpose of the church). I want the church to be an agent of transformation in the world. Jesus came to bring about a completely new social and cultural order. It is an order grounded in love and self-sacrifice with Jesus at the center. This new order will bring about reconciliation where there is strife, peace and healing where there has been violence, and repentance where there has been wickedness. Yes, the church is called to have power to bring about these kinds of changes in the larger society, but it does so through its healthy patterns of worship and witness. As mentioned in previous pages, worship has the power to transform individuals and societies. This power comes not in worship that soothes us and affirms us, but in worship that draws us to vigorous repentance, humble study of Scripture, and then Holy Spirit empowerment. A healthy church may look meek, mild, and harmless, but it contains the power for change that *all* of the world and *each* person needs.

The second question, Who is Jesus? needs to be a constant part of our Christian life.[3] We do not reach an answer to this by sitting in a library or doing a Google search. That would be entertaining, but not faithful to the Jesus of history, who is the Son of God. No. We answer this question together as we take Jesus at his word. We live into the answer of who Jesus is, because the answer to this question comes in our own lives. We are being transformed into his likeness. Therefore, who Jesus is has to do with who I am becoming and what the church is becoming in Christ. What do I mean?

If the answer to this question about Jesus comes through the life of the Christian community, through our life together studying Scripture and worshiping together, then we can see some of the answer in the lives of others. Haven't you known people who exemplify for you what it really means to be a Christian, people who seem to shine with the glory of Christ in the way they act and how they speak? I know I have. I have been fortunate to know a number of these people. It is not their personality, for some of these people are extroverts and some are introverts. Some are artistic and poetic, and others are engineers and left-brain analytical types. Each in their own way exemplifies something of Christ for others to see and experience. One of those persons was my advisor in my PhD program, Dr. Samuel Hugh Moffett. Gentle but firm, kind but penetrating in his analysis, I always came to his house or office prepared and I always left thankful. In his relationships with others, in his marriage, in his teaching and writing, he exemplified humility. When I was a young scholar he supported me and opened doors for me even though I don't believe I deserved it. There have been others too.

Our answer to both of these questions comes together. We learn about who Jesus is as we work at becoming the body of Christ (the Church). It is in the local church that we practice the presence and life of Christ for others and for the world. It is important to keep these questions together and to continue to ask them as part of our life together.

PART OF AND WITNESS TO . . .

Any local church, a gathering of people centered on Jesus Christ, is both *part of* a local community and is at the same time a *witness to* that community. This means that if the local community is a rural farm area, we would expect to see local farmers, landowners, and laborers (adults as well as children) in the local church. The local church should reflect the local community. If the local church is located in Pasadena, California (where I lived), we would expect to see local people from the neighborhood. Thus, we would find many Hispanics, African Americans, Euro-Americans, Armenians, Koreans, and other Asian Americans. That is the make-up the neighborhoods I passed when I rode my bike to work. The church should be a reconciling community bringing together people who are united in Jesus Christ, even if they are not united in many other ways.

Although Pasadena is multicultural, it is common knowledge that certain groups choose to stay together and stay away from other groups. There is an Armenian area, a mostly Hispanic area, and a predominately African American area in Pasadena. It reminds me of my junior high

school lunchtime and of the student union at my university. People
choose to be with people they are like. On one level this is fine and it is
important. Some examples may help. Koreans hang together because
they speak Korean and have particular Korean parents issues. Hispanics often share common issues of relating to their home country and
dealing with issues of work visas, children learning English, and concerns
related to employment. So we should not be too critical of homogenous
groups staying together.

However, the church should bring these groups together into the
church and then work to break down the divisions between various
groups. If we only have homogenous groups in our culture, we breed
racism and injustices. The church must resist this, becoming a signpost
to the larger culture of what can and should happen in human societies.
We should expect and even embrace the diversity of cultures, races, economic class, ages, genders, and abilities. The church is called to break
down walls of partition and to build a community of love.

Here we have just one example of how each local church is both part
of the local culture (in my case very multicultural and multilinguistic),
and a witness to that culture (in resisting segregation). I asked one of the
local pastors of a very large church in Pasadena how many different language services they have each week. "I am not really sure," he said. He
knew of a fairly large Spanish-speaking service, an Arabic service, and
one in Mandarin, but he thought they also had a Cantonese service and a
Korean service. His is a single church speaking the languages of local
immigrants and including them in a single church body that carries out
mission as a multicultural body.

This same church is also part of the local community and a witness to
that community in the way they care for adults with disabilities. They
have a special adult class on Sundays and activities during the week for
these adults. We do not have an adult child with such special needs, but
I am sure if we did we would just love to live near this church. Imagine:
a local church who cares for your adult child, understands her or his
limitations and special giftedness, and lovingly cares for him or her while
speaking of Jesus. These adults are *part of* every community, and

the church should find ways of embracing them and ministering to them—which becomes a witness to the larger society. There are many other ways that a healthy church both reflects the local culture(s) and is a witness to that culture.

TWO STRUCTURES IN THE CHRISTIAN MOVEMENT

In writing this chapter I was also researching the history of Christianity in Asia. On one hand, Christianity in China is so very different from the history and life of Christianity in North America or even South America. In the Americas, most of the people who settled and later dominated the territory were Christian with Christian rulers. Therefore, churches were established ("planted") in most new villages, cities, and territories. What we often forget is that the early history of Christianity in places like Texas, New Orleans, California, or even Quebec was built around monastic settlements and/or schools, clinics, and orphanages. These monasteries were not churches. The schools were not churches, but they related very closely to the churches. Soon churches sprang up where these monasteries or clinics or orphanages first started.

In fact, (historian that I am) this was the case in the development of churches in Europe and across Russia and in many parts of Africa and South Asia. Christian schools (or monasteries) were the pioneers, and churches later followed. Would it be acceptable (according to our understanding of Scripture) if only schools were started, with no church? No, this would be an incomplete mission. God's mission, started in Jesus Christ, is to bring communities to faith (trust in Jesus) to be worshiping communities with the marks talked about in the preceding chapters. A school (or clinic or orphanage) is not a place of gathering, of praising, and of confessing. It has a different purpose and a different (highly selective) community.

Still, these nonchurch Christian institutions—called sodalities[4]—work with the local church or churches, but have complementary purposes. They have a more limited purpose, more focused community, and less diverse functions. Think of it this way. A local church (maybe your church) wants to reach out to unchurched young people coming to a local college or university. The university has 15,000 undergraduates and 6,000 graduate students. The church has 250 members; only eight members are free during the day. The rest are working, looking after children, or are in school themselves. How are these young university students going to be reached for Jesus? A sodality is developed that focuses only on reaching university students. Local churches provide support, open their homes, and welcome the new Christians into their worship services and discipleship classes. Eight or fifteen local churches may support this massive effort to reach a university. The sodality, which is like a parachurch organization (university Christian outreach) dovetails with the local church (called a modality).

Sodality and modality are two basic structures of Christianity that have existed since Paul's missionary band and Peter's church in Jerusalem. In Christian history the main outreach of the church has always been done by sodalities: monasteries, Bible societies, mission societies, student fellowship groups, Christian schools, and Christian relief agencies.

I learned from missionary work in Asia that churches were often planted through sodalities, but sodalities were never the goal or the end in sight. Today I know of many churches started as sodalities. Here are a few that I have known personally:

- Local theater or drama group
- Financial advising center
- Marriage and family counseling center
- Basketball league outreach for youth
- Coffee shop and poetry reading
- Prayer house
- Homeless shelter
- Home evangelistic Bible study
- Preschool center
- Informal creative music center
- After-school tutoring and arts center for youth

I am sure you can think of many others. Each of these is meeting some type of need in the community, but then they extend or expand the focused activities and begin to develop a church. It is quite appropriate and it may even be important for a local church to either start from a sodality like those mentioned above or, after a church has existed for a while, it might develop particular ministries that create their own sodality. Developing a missional sodality begins with the local church praying about being attentive to the particular needs around them, as well as the needs in the world. How do we move out? Will it require a new structure (sodality)? A new church will likely emerge from this missional structure, a normal process of church planting.

YOU DON'T CHOOSE YOUR FAMILY

In junior high school, an important social event that shapes a young adolescent is lunchtime: what table will you sit at? The same is true in high school. We chose to identify with certain people (musicians, athletes, geeks, etc.) or a group we would like to identify with may or may not select us. It can be a very stressful moment, coming into a cafeteria. I remember well, even in my old age, going into the high school cafeteria. Although hot lunches were sold, I always brought in some sort of hoagie or a PB and J. Chips and an apple completed my lunch diet for close to twelve years of schooling.

As I walked through the doors, I would look to the left and see my friends from choir class, which just ended. They were older than I, a little geeky (none played sports), but we were friends. Often I would sit with them. But to my right were my friends from the soccer team. We had just won a key game and I scored a rare goal. It was time to debrief and bask in the light of victory. And then there was the really geeky table. I did not think of myself as a great student, but somehow I got in National Honor Society, and that was another table in the cafeteria. Torn between three tables, I was still choosing my friends. I was choosing my community, which, conversely, would shape me.

A church is not like that—even though we too often assume it is. A church is not like a high school cafeteria or a college fraternity or sorority. A church, if you are in an urban neighborhood, is a local gathering of people knit together as a family. They come together as a community because Jesus is there. The same is true in a small village. The church is there. If you just came to faith or just moved to the village, you become part of this family. In such a context, you are stuck with people you did not choose. This is the beauty and grace, as well as the tension and the pain, of the church. Families are like that.

At this point I think it is good to consider Jesus and his disciples. Jesus chose his disciples and then each disciple turned around and looked and found they had a community of really close friends that they did not choose. My guess is that some of the quieter disciples were not happy to be identified with Peter, always quick to answer, often before thinking. Still, Jesus called them each, and he called them together.

Unconditional love, unconventional community. Our family attended a suburban church where the youth represented two local school districts and most of the families shopped at two major grocery chains. Because the church had a preschool, many of the children started their schooling in a church taught by some church members. Friday night football games as well as Tuesday or Thursday evening soccer games were a good time to find the pastor, church secretary, some elders from the church; all were cheering on the team, but especially the church members, whether on the bench or quarterbacking the team to victory (or more frequently defeats). During basketball season there always seemed to be one or two church members on the varsity and the junior varsity teams, so church members could be found in the stands cheering and catching up on church news. Some of the planning for mission trips took place in the stands!

> When we come to Jesus, we come to his community and we become responsible to love these (often) unlovely people.

It was not idyllic, for some of the young people from the church got in trouble. Not all were stars on the teams or soloists in the choir or part of band concerts. But the church, as a community, was there for them and to meet their friends from the team or the band. Some of those friends joined the church. I coached a community soccer team, and a father and his son later joined the church. We were an unconventional community, but offered (as much as we could) unconditional love. It was attractive to many people.

At this same church was a man in his fifties who was a little slow mentally. He was single, worked at a local grocery store and also mowed some lawns in a rather generic or impressionistic manner. Johnny would come to church early, greet everyone in a very extroverted (loud) manner and would be a little too chummy with some of the women. He sat in the back of the church and often had prayer requests he would vocalize. Everyone knew Johnny because he brought them their grocery carts at the grocery store, mowed their lawns and, well, it was hard not to know him! Johnny had a mother who lived in a home for the elderly, and that was his whole family. Actually, the church was his family. We prayed for him, talked to him, invited him to church suppers, and someone took him to the doctor when he was sick. Everyone knew Johnny, and he was happy as could be with his family.

A local church, as the body of Jesus Christ, has unconditional love for others, and because of this, it develops an unconventional community. Unconditional love is grounded in its worship, but it is the kind of love that attracts very needy people. In fact, a good and healthy church will have a larger number of people who have had a hard time fitting in elsewhere.

There will be more people with needs, but as they become involved in the church they move from being people of need to people with gifts to serve others. A healthy church unconditionally loves people with emotional wounds or psychiatric illnesses, people without full mobility or sight or hearing, those without jobs or homes.

Two other groups are also unconditionally loved: children and the elderly. Both children and the elderly generally have more needs than the average person. They are not able to give as much as other people. But the church has unconditional love for children and for the elderly.

A church worship service, or any church activity, should be a place that children love to come to. We have had that experience and it is just wonderful. When children can't wait to go to church, or to a fellowship meeting, they are experiencing something of the unconditional love from Jesus that they will someday give to others.

The same is true of the elderly and the infirm. A healthy church unconditionally loves the elderly. A number of years ago our pastor was on vacation and I was called on to visit a man in the hospital. All I was told was his name and the name of his wife. They were in their late seventies, and he was dying of cancer. No children lived in the area. They were alone, and they were estranged from the church. They had not attended for over a decade. Still, at this difficult time, they asked for a pastoral visit. They were all alone. I prayed and showed up.

I quickly assessed the situation. He was dying (cold, thin, looking gray in the face), and she was in denial. After a few moments she gathered up some courage and said, "When we get out of this hospital, we are going to start going back to church." I knew he would not get out of the hospital, so I decided we needed to talk about Jesus. I pulled out my Bible and read some verses. I prayed for them. I laid my hands on the dying man and prayed for his soul. Two days later he passed and we did a small memorial service for this man, estranged from most of his family, but cared for by the church. The church came around the widow, bringing meals, inviting her to worship and then to a small group. She ended up attending almost every meeting or gathering that was held. When the church doors were open, she was there. She could not get enough of this community that had shown her such love.

Little churches. A healthy church understands and cultivates small communities within the church. A remarkable movement in Protestant Christianity called Pietism originated in Germany in the seventeenth and eighteenth centuries. During a time when Christian life was often preoccupied with differences (Presbyterians don't have bishops; Catholics have a central authority in the papacy, etc.), the Pietist movement in Germany spread through the focus on devotion to Christ through small groups. It was a movement, too; it spread beyond the Lutheran churches

in Germany to influence some Reformed churches, and it was foundational in the rise of Methodism. One of the keys was small groups from
a local church meeting in the evening in church members' homes to
study the Sunday sermon or to study a Bible passage. They were not
rogue groups, but they were very much like small churches as part of
a local congregation. In fact, they were called a "small church in
the church."[5]

Since the 1960s modern Western churches have recovered much of
this—a very good thing, I think. In fact, I think it is essential for a healthy
church to have these types of gatherings. A look at the early church
should make it obvious that this is the normal Christian pattern. Jesus
informally developed two structures (if we can call it this) to his
movement. First, he intentionally chose twelve to be close to him to hear
the backstory of parables, healings, and other miracles. The twelve were
his small group. They were committed not only to Jesus, but also to each
other, and these commitments continued after Jesus was taken
from them.

Second, Jesus had the crowds. Many in the crowds were genuinely
converted followers. Others were followers for the big show, and Jesus
knew that. Still larger groups gathered for church suppers (feeding of the
5,000) and for sermons (Sermon on the Mount). Jesus was pleased to
reach more and more people, and so he spoke to the crowds, and he
moved from town to town, and he even crossed lakes and preached by
the shore. His movement had minimal structure.

The earliest gatherings of Christians met in homes and in the synagogues. However, they were quickly pushed out of the synagogues (this
was not just a Jewish sect), but they still met in small groups in homes.
Some of the home gatherings were large (over 100), but most were small
because the homes were small. For centuries most Christian gatherings
met in homes; this tells us a lot about the life and practice and teaching
of Christianity at its foundation. The earliest followers of Jesus established,
both by necessity and choice, a small group structure similar to Jesus and
the disciples. These differed in that these groups were even more closely
rooted in home and community life. Where Jesus chose twelve men, the

earliest little house churches consisted of families, couples, and singles from the local community.

Little church purposes. Again, I believe every church should have some small group structure for every church member and even for those on the fringes of the church. The following basic purposes for these little churches should make it clear why small groups are essential to the local church.

1. In the small group we know each other by name and we *look into each other's eyes.* In most congregations (not all) we all look at the back of others' heads and maybe we look at the pastor or priest and a few other church leaders. In a small group, we usually sit in a circle of some sort and talk to each other about heavenly things. This is very important because, unlike some other religions based upon ritual practices, in the Church, we are brought into relationship with the living God and with each other.

All barriers have been broken down, so we can and should look at each other. The following purpose will show why this is important.

2. In a small group we can obey the injunction to *confess your sins to one another* (Jas 5:16). We are commanded to do this, but it is not really feasible to do so on Sunday morning (think of how long the service would be!), and few churches have the practice of confessing to a priest. Christian faith, at its root, requires confession for what we have done to separate us from God. God has already offered forgiveness and acceptance, but we need to admit our need. Prayer is surrender, and surrender requires admitting that we can't do it; that we have already erred. It is hard enough to even admit our mistakes, but the only way forward in the Christian faith is on our knees, and this means confession. Thus, a small group can complete what was begun in chapter five when we confessed during worship.

3. In a small group we can *bring healing to one another through the power of the Holy Spirit.* When we confess our inadequacies and our pain and our wounds, we have in that little church others who, though also wounded, have the Holy Spirit in them to provide

solace, advice, and prayers for healing. Memories are flooding my mind of the many times our small groups in the past have prayed for healing, provided spiritual guidance, and wept together over sufferings of our brothers and sisters in our little church. We became very close in these times of caring for each other. We have been in small groups where a person was diagnosed with a terminal disease, had a spouse who died, someone needed a pacemaker, a parent was dying, a member had a severe handicap, and someone had a mental illness. And the struggles continue. Children get married, and children fail out of school. We lose our job, or we do not get the raise we had hoped for. Basements flood, and children get in accidents. In all of life's pains, the family, with the support of the Christian community, is available to provide support. Of course, these burdens belong to the whole church, but we need to be loved in personal ways by people with whom we have built trust. The little church is the first, and at times, the only place where such support and healing can occur.

4. It is in the little church where the *teachings of Scripture and the message of the sermon are applied.* The Bible is not a private document, as if the pastor as guru gives us a private chant. No, the Bible is a public document, and the sermon is for the whole congregation. Every one of us is responsible to live into Christ as we study his Word. If we read John 15 in our own devotion or hear it read in a worship service, we are responsible to live into this teaching that Jesus is the vine and we are the branches. What does this mean in general, and what does this mean specifically to and for me this week? In a small church we can ask these questions and then help each other remain faithful. It is very appropriate to bring up the question the next week—and the next week, How are we being faithful to being branches of Jesus, and how have we been disobedient to this teaching? Again, on a personal level we can help one another follow Jesus in specific ways from specific teaching.

5. The small group *can be very evangelistic*. Most little churches meet in homes and homes are usually in apartments, condominiums, duplexes, or freestanding houses. We have neighbors who see people coming into the house for our small church gathering. Assuming we know our neighbors (an important assumption) it is often easier to invite a neighbor into our living room than to a church building. More and more we will find in the West that our neighbors have no experience of going to a worship service, and it may seem intimidating to them. However, if we have been good neighbors, the people who live around us should know they are welcome in our yard and in our home. Hospitality is an important dimension of Christian witness or mission. Not all little churches will be evangelistic, but most should be. There are times when the needs of the group or the fragile nature of some of our pains and personal issues require us to stay together to care for each other. However, we should always look for the day when we can, once again, feel free to invite in our neighbors to see something of Jesus in the little church life.

6. The little church is also *the place of mission preparation and sending*. Not only local evangelism, but even global mission can find its foundation in the little church. As we study Scripture together, we learn that Christian life in Jesus Christ is a missional life. If we are in Christ we are living our life in the life of Jesus, the missionary of God. Thus, we begin to look for ways to live into that mission. As I mentioned before, Nancy and I were in a small group once that learned of the need for families and churches to sponsor Vietnamese refugee families. So it was that our small group of twenty-somethings learned to sacrifice for refugees and learned to cross cultural boundaries in presenting Christ and his love. It was also in that small group that we affirmed our call to serve in Asia, where we later served for eight years. In the little church we discuss our local issues of homelessness, issues with local schools, treatment of the elderly, drug trafficking in our neighborhoods, illiteracy, or whatever issues

we become aware of. Attentiveness, with the eyes and mind of Christ, is the beginning of our mission involvement that has its genesis in our neighborhood and its goal to reach all the nations.

These are the basic purposes of small groups in general. However, not all little churches are small groups that meet in homes. Larger churches will have other types of small groups that can serve many of the same purposes. We should not try to apply a one-size-fits-all approach to little churches in the big church. When people are serving the church in important ways, through the choir, worship team, Sunday school, or in other structures, it is not necessary to require more meetings ("Oh, don't you know, you also have to be in one of our small groups."). No, let these other service groups in the church function as little churches, with just a little guidance and lots of prayer.

Other little churches. Other affinity groups (often service groups) will naturally develop in a local church, and these can strengthen the church and its witness to its parish or community. For example, young mothers and pregnant young women find it easy to build relationships of trust. When this happens, a church should affirm the needs being met, and then come alongside and suggest some guidelines, or at least a broader sense of purpose, so these affinity groups become an integral part of the local church. Here are some examples:

1. Youth and children's groups[6]

2. Choir and/or worship team

3. Men

4. Singles

5. Young mothers

6. Unemployed

7. Leadership team (session, board, etc.)

8. Recovery groups

In this sample of the types of groups that often form in healthy churches, each has a particular mission or purpose, yet they still should exemplify the larger church in life of worship and mission. A few examples may help. The leadership team (session, board, vestry, etc.) should study the Bible together and should pray for one another. If one of their members is in the hospital, others should visit them and pray for them. We do not have to wait for the pastor to initiate this type of care. The small group cares for one another, and it is centered on Scripture.

In a similar way, your church may develop a ministry for those coming out of addictions. In fact, given the rate of alcohol, drug, and other addictions today, I think every church should have this ministry. When someone in the recovery group is having trouble with their marriage, or with their children, or getting a job, the small group should function as a healthy little church, caring for each person. Scripture should be read, discussed, and prayed over. In short, every small group in a church should have a healthy Christian life about it. No need to have special small groups. Make sure that every group that meets is aware of their wholesome calling to Christ and to each other. Look each other in the eyes and confess Christ and his love to each other. Nothing will kill a healthy church faster than allowing task-oriented groups to lose their spiritual calling in all that they do.

WORSHIP IS THE BASIC TRAINING IN THE FAITH

My slow drifting away from the church as a teenager, I believed, was caused in part by the unhealthy condition of my church. Worship services were almost meaningless to me. I had no idea what the Gloria Patri was (or why we sang it when we did and how we did) and the meaning of Eucharist also escaped me. I remember on the Communion table (altar for Roman Catholics) was carved the following: "This do in remembrance of me." When I was about sixteen years old, I found that Jesus said these very words at the Last Supper. I had to piece together what it all meant. Most of it was not a divine mystery; it was just confusing.

This is not the way worship is supposed to be. Worship is to be instructive and have a tending function. Like a shepherd guiding sheep or a master guiding an apprentice, worship should guide us into deeper understanding of and life in Jesus Christ.

We worship with our mind engaged, our eyes wide open, and our hearts tender. A Roman Catholic missionary who worked among the Maasai in East Africa, Vincent J. Donovan, described this very well. He noticed that 90 percent of the young Maasai Christians were being educated (catechized) by young people who were poorly educated. Christian character and Christian virtues were not being developed. In fact, the Maasai continued to revere revenge more than mercy or forgiveness. They thought that sin required a fine to be paid to God. And God seemed so distant and far off that they continued to pray to the ancestors for help. This was the teaching they were given by the local Christian teachers. The work of reeducating a whole generation of young people seemed impossible. So, Father Donovan decided that the worship service or the liturgy (see below on liturgy) should teach the young what it meant to be truly Christian. In this way, services every week would reinforce the true meaning of Christian life. A separate school or discipleship center would not be needed.[7]

Worship is a main purpose for the church, and in worship we are educated, trained, or shaped to think more like Jesus, to empathize more like Jesus, and to act more like Jesus. Worship should be the basic discipleship of the church. Adult education and Sunday schools are a modern phenomenon, probably developed because worship became less meaningful. However, the whole service—from coming to standing to kneeling to sitting to going—all is an educational endeavor. In a healthy church these movements, and all that we do, should be explained so all can participate with joyful meaning. We should explain that the Eucharist or Lord's Supper follows preaching as a response to the words of Scripture. We enter and sing songs of praise and thanksgiving because God has *already* acted on our behalf. We don't need to wake up God or bribe him to do something for us; he has already loved us even when we were far off in our sin. Healthy worship is meaningful worship through and through.

BEAUTY OF LITURGY: LITURGY AS A MURAL OF WORSHIP

We have waited a long time in this book to talk about something that is so central to the majority of churches in the world. I have held off because my hope is that most of the people reading this book are asking more basic questions about what the church is or should be. Therefore, churchy language (*ecclesial* means "church"; *eschatology* means "the last things," etc.) has been reduced to a bare minimum. But as we move into the last pages of the book, we need to become aware that most churches in the world (Roman Catholic, Anglican, Orthodox, Lutheran, etc.) do not choose each week how to worship. They have a prescribed, often ancient, liturgy or program (form) for weekly worship. Like the magnificent mural in the Sistine Chapel, or the ceiling fresco in the same chapel, liturgy is a mural that tells the story of salvation for us, centered on the life and work of Jesus Christ.

Liturgy is an ancient Greek concept for public duty or a public work. This duty (before the time of Jesus Christ) could be public service, but it became synonymous with priestly functions in pagan worship. In the Old Testament the priest's work in the temple was considered liturgy (literally "people" + "duty/work"). In the New Testament, this practice became the work of church leaders in leading worship. Slowly, agreed-upon rhythms in worship and patterns of prayers and of the Eucharistic celebration developed. By the end of the second century, basic patterns had been established to guide Christians throughout the Roman and Persian empires. When divisions arose over the life and meaning of Jesus, it was worship that helped to keep the church united.[8]

All churches have liturgies, whether they are very formal and published for priests and pastors to follow (the Roman Catholic missal or the Anglican *Book of Common Prayer*), or they are informal and not even put in print. Anyone who has attended a particular Pentecostal church for a few months realizes that they have a pattern of worship or a liturgy. Most newly planted churches follow a liturgy, and new visitors quickly pick it up. Some common elements are the use of the Lord's Prayer, the language of Jesus and Paul for celebration of the Lord's Supper, and most churches in the world use the Apostles' Creed or the Nicene Creed occasionally or weekly. Most churches use biblical prayers and blessings, and many use the Aaronic blessing from Numbers 6:24-26. Such common practices remind us what holds us together: Jesus and Holy Scripture.

Here I am not arguing for accepting a particular liturgy, but I do think it is important for churches that have not discussed their pattern of worship or liturgy to ask themselves, What is our assumed liturgy? What do we do each week, and why do we do it? Then it may be helpful to look at the liturgies or worship books of other churches for some common features that would enrich the worship and help to teach the congregation more about God.

RHYTHMS AND SEASONS OF LIFE

A healthy local church is a community that interprets, celebrates, and mourns the cycles and vicissitudes of life. I remember like it was yesterday the enormous increase in attendance in churches after the 9/11 attacks on the World Trade Center in New York and the Pentagon in Washington, DC. People were confused and they were looking for answers. Church leaders were warned that it was a temporary upsurge in church attendance, but it did show the need for the local church community to be a place to gather in the midst of tragedy or confusion or loss. We are made for patterns, rhythms, and rituals. Jesus instituted some rituals for us, and in the Old Testament God instituted rituals (as well as fasts and feasts) and laws to live by, to give our lives brief rest stops to get off the highway of life and reflect and rest. These rituals also give us signs that point to a better understanding of great mysteries around suffering, birth, marriage, and death. I am so glad for the church as we celebrated weddings of our children as well as births and baptisms. I have personally been so very grateful for the church at periods of loss and transitions in life. The Church, through local churches, has been for us the place of comfort and counsel in times of loss.

Lament and longing. The first two funerals I did, when I was just thirty-four and thirty-five years old, were for a young father who died of

AIDS and a late teen who committed suicide. Both were terrible experiences. Since the time of these two experiences in Asia, I have done the funeral of my mother, my sister, and my niece, among many others. Death and suffering are uninvited guests in God's beautiful and joyful world. How do we endure and how do we move on from such experiences? We do so with our local congregation as our extended family and as Jesus' mystical presence.

The suicide death—my first funeral—in East Asia was an eighteen-year-old Chinese woman who became depressed when her boyfriend rejected her. She became despondent and, before people had a chance to encourage her to get some help, she climbed up to the fifteenth story of her apartment building and jumped off. Her family was Buddhist, and she was the only Christian. I did not speak Hokkien (a Chinese dialect), so the funeral and counsel for the family had to be done through a translator. It was an awful situation. However, at the graveside funeral I spoke to the parents, brother, and sister-in-law about Jesus, and I gave them a Chinese Bible. The church members visited the family every night for over a month, bringing food, telling stories, reading the Bible, and praying with them. Lamenting the death of the young girl, this Buddhist family discovered the comfort and resurrection power of Jesus Christ. They all became Christians, and the next spring I baptized the brother, sister-in-law, and their new baby in the English-language service. The Chinese pastor baptized the parents the same day in the Hokkien service.

The pains and sufferings in this life, at times, are overwhelming. The church is the presence of Christ at such times. We are encouraged to pray the Psalms, to express our anger, our pain, and our confusion to God. God can handle it. He expects us to come to him. He understands an unjust and violent death. He understands loneliness and abandonment. So, as a church we come together in times of pain and loss. The persistent questions are usually best answered in the presence of the community, not in the reasoning of Why me? Why now?

In the church as the body of Christ, suffering and death are embraced, and we are allowed to live in the loss together. Jesus is acquainted with grief and suffering; we have a God who is not distant, but who walks with us through the darkness of suffering and death: "Even though I walk through the darkest valley, I will fear no evil, for you are with me" (Ps 23:4). When any person or family suffers, the church is the larger family that takes

> A healthy church is not repulsed by pain and suffering. It is a place that welcomes weeping.

them in, comforts them, and stays by their side. If you have not experienced this yet, at some point in your life you will experience such loss and pain. When this happens, your family will need greater resources to receive both the comfort and the guidance for how to move forward. The church is filled with healers who have also been wounded, people who have been scarred but are now strong.

Joy and celebration. A healthy church is also a place of celebration and joy. Sometimes it is both in the same week. Five years ago my father died on a Sunday and our son got married the next Saturday. From Colorado to New York I flew across two time zones from grief and crying to joy and celebration. A patriarch had died and a new family was born. Churches absorb the pain and then magnify the celebration. Both are healthy responses to life this side of Eden.

We need to make more of joy in the Christian life—in fact, in all of life. The word *joy*, along with the verbal command "rejoice," is used about 375 times in the Bible.[9] This is remarkable. Imagine a God who talks so much about joy! We are even commanded to rejoice. Joy is not a forced emotion ("Son, you better smile when you see your mother!"); it is a natural response to fellowship with the living God and with his kingdom people. I am thinking a lot about joy now since we have ten grandchildren. When one is born, Nancy cashes in some extra miles from an airline and heads for the city where the new child is born. Soon I have pictures sent to me with a beaming Mimi (each grandmother must have a special name) holding a precious little miracle. The siblings and the aunts and uncles all want to get in the face of the baby and kiss the little cheeks. Babies elicit joy.

God has such joy with each person who is saved and with each new life that is born. God loves life. How wonderful that God gives us a wedding, and specifically a wedding banquet, as an image of heaven. Our life with God is like a grand party filled with joy, celebration, and hope. At weddings we put our daily cares and concerns on hold, and we face each other and say, "Let's celebrate!" In Matthew 22:1-14, Jesus condemns those who are too preoccupied to enjoy a free wedding banquet—and those who are not prepared properly. In Jesus' first miracle, recorded in John 2:1-12, he provides more wine for a wedding feast, and not just wine, but superior tasting wine. Quality and quantity matter when it comes to celebration. It was a wedding with great joy.

> Church is a place where we can celebrate with great joy and not feel guilty. Our celebration is always a thanksgiving, for all that we have is from God and it is given to us freely.

We have four children and all are married. We have had four weddings (plus we have celebrated weddings of cousins over the past decade). Each wedding has been a celebration with laughter, meeting new people, learning about families (which is always fun), and for some of the celebrations, wine and dancing. We tell stories now about the great celebrations, and we have pictures to help us tell those stories better. "Do you remember Elisha's best man's speech?" and then we all laugh again.

I would like to suggest that much of the joy in weddings and other celebrations in the church is in meeting new people, looking at them in the face and increasing our fellowship. There is great joy in relationships, and Jesus' great work is all about reconciling people with God and with one another.

Joy and sorrow, laughter and lamentation. It may seem odd that the church is both the place where we can have healthy lament and be full of joy and celebration. But think about this: both the Old and New Testaments identify Jesus with both sorrow and joy. He is both the "Man of sorrows" (Is 53:3 NKJV) and the one who said, "I have told you this so that my joy may be in you and that your joy may be complete" (Jn 15:11). A healthy church encourages people to come with their pain and to come with their joy.

ALL FOR THE GLORY OF CHRIST

The church is to be a place where we use our best gifts and most honed talents for the worship of God and witness to God. What exactly does this mean? If I work as an accountant and have developed respected skills in accounts and finances I can (maybe should) give these gifts to the local church. Can a church use a good accountant? You bet. If I am an artist and I create artwork for plays, for local public buildings, or I am an art teacher, I should ask, "Could the church use my talent?" Absolutely. As early as the tabernacle that God directed Moses to have built in the wilderness we have evidence of artistry and craftsmanship as part of worship. Throughout the history of the church, artists have expressed the message of the Bible and even the specific stories of Jesus and the patriarchs. Art has also been used for Christian witness as people see the paintings, sculptures, or buildings and give glory to God.

What about the teacher, the salesman, the carpenter, or the landscape architect? Yes, yes, and yes. In the church and through the church, all of these people need to know that their gifts and skills should be offered to serve Jesus Christ through the church. All.

A number of churches I have attended list the various staff employed by the church and then they list under "Ministers": All Church Members. This is a helpful reminder. Each and every person is called to be a witness and to give all of her or his life to Jesus.

At a seminar for a regional body of churches in New Jersey many years ago, I was leading one on evangelism. I was saying that everything God has built into our lives can be, or should be, blessed to help others come to know Christ. One man, with a very low view of himself said, "Frankly, I do not have anything special that can be used to reach others for Jesus." I felt I was on pretty solid ground here, so I simply asked him, "Tell me about what you do for a job and what you like to do in your spare time." I don't remember his job except that it did sound boring, but then he said

> A healthy church helps people find how each person can invest their lives in God's kingdom work.

he likes to play chess. Our small group talked about how God might use this, and very quickly we suggested that he start a chess club at the local junior high school. He did this and soon young men were visiting him at church. Families came to see what type of man would give up his free time to spend with junior high boys. They found a wonderful man who loved Jesus.

All that we are and all that we have is to be laid at the feet of Jesus.

SO WHAT IS IN A NAME? (REVISITED)

An often-repeated story has been told about the great eighteenth-century preacher George Whitefield. Preaching in the open air, concerned about all the divisions among Christians, he turned his gaze up toward heaven and shouted out:

> "Father Abraham, are there any Anglicans in heaven?" The answer came back, "No, there are no Anglicans in heaven." "Father Abraham, are there any Methodists in heaven?" "No, there are no Methodists in heaven." "Are there any Presbyterians in heaven?" "No, there are no Presbyterians here either." "What about Baptists or Quakers?" "No, there are none of those here either." "Father Abraham," cried Whitefield, "what kind of people are in heaven?" The answer came back, "There are only Christians in heaven; only those who are washed in the blood of the Lamb." Whitefield then cried out, "Oh, is that the case? Then God help me, God help us all, to forget having names and to become Christians in deed and in truth!"[10]

In chapter one we looked at the amazing array of names for churches, each identifying what the founders considered important to communicate to others about their community. Whitefield—and myself as well—was less concerned about specific names and more concerned about the common identity. In a world of divisions and insecurities about losing our identity (because of immigrants, globalization, etc.), the Church and each local church must be clear that the only identity that matters is the full identification with and life in Jesus Christ. Divisions must give way to unity and suspicions must yield to grace. A healthy church will cultivate such an attitude. Have this mind in you that was in Christ Jesus (Phil 2:5). That mindset of humility will bring about unity in Jesus Christ. Amen.

EPILOGUE
What We Did Not Talk About

A BOOK LIKE THIS USUALLY has two diametrically opposed results. A thoughtful reader may put this down and say, "That is so depressing! I would love to find a church like this, but there is no such thing. This makes me even more disappointed with my church (or the churches I have been visiting). I like what he says, but there is no church like this. It is hopeless."

Or a (glass is half full) person may say, "Yes! That is what I thought the church is supposed to be like! I am going to share this with my pastor and see if we can talk about this together! Maybe we can have an adult education class on this and talk about how we make decisions about our church. I now have some hope for our church to move forward."

I have had a number of people read every chapter of this for me, to give me feedback on whether it communicates well to Pentecostals, Episcopalians, lay people, Hispanics, African Americans, women, pastors, and so forth. Their comments have been very helpful, but they too hint at the problem with setting up an ideal type of the church. We may all be depressed after reading this. I hope not.

SO, HOW DO I THINK ABOUT WHAT I HAVE READ?

I have not really talked about the nature or essence of the church. That seems a little too theoretical. However, as I conclude, let me suggest a way to think about why churches give us such joy and such anguish—and how to think about what you have read: a local church is both human and divine.

> A local church
> is both human
> and divine.

Some really miraculous things happen in a local church. Marriages are healed in the midst of a culture that says fidelity is overrated. Young people dedicate their lives to serving the poor when social media says serve yourself and love yourself above all. Homeless people are loved, and people of different races and economic classes come together to serve others. Orphans are adopted. These are wonderful and miraculous signs of the presence of Jesus' kingdom for a narcissistic world. I have seen these types of miracles in many places in the world, and I hope you have seen some yourself. Maybe you received such uncommon and remarkable love yourself.

However, in churches that we *thought* were really wonderful, we also find that pastors get too full of themselves and they begin to think they are above others. They compromise the church morally and ethically. Churches turn against their leaders and against each other because of moral failure. We attend churches that think the music is the church (only the music) or that teaching is the church (only teaching), or that protecting someone's self-esteem is more important than speaking the truth. We are really broken and weak people. It is amazing that God still cares about the Church. But he does.

This analogy might help. A parent is describing her or his daughter to a distant relative and, as should be the case, tells about how sweet she is, how well she is doing in school and then tells about a recent mission trip she went on and how it changed her life. Does she tell about how last year she was caught smoking behind the school, or how she "borrowed" twenty dollars from her mother's purse to buy beer? This wonderful daughter is also an adolescent who is making great progress in following Christ, but is still a *work in progress*. She is like all of us, both very human but with the living God at work in her life. Since these are good parents, they lift up for their daughter models of what she may grow up to be. They expose her to really good people who have done amazing things. They open Scriptures to her so God's Spirit can speak to her soul. She, like the church, is human, with the image of God impressed on her soul.

So, as an epilogue to this book, let me suggest some perspectives, some ways of thinking about your church and this book.

A VISION IS NECESSARY

Today we need a vision of what the church should be, what it is meant to be, and what it can be. We have plenty of ideas, experiments, and blogs about the church. I believe we need a common shared vision that pulls us forward, that guides us. We need both unity and integrity in concert. A coach, when training a gifted athlete, does not start by saying, "Wow! You are a great athlete! Just relax and show up for the game. I am sure, with your great talent you will go to the state finals." That would be foolish. The coach should affirm potential, but then the coach needs to cast a vision for the athlete. "The training this year will not be without moments of joy, but it will be hard. You are going to have to focus; cut out junk food. Get eight or nine hours of sleep a night. Work hard six days a week and take one day off with no training at all." Then the coach, after talking about the hard work says, "I think you will be jumping 23 feet by the end of the spring." Or, "Let's plan on going to the state meet. If you stay healthy and follow the plan I have for you, I am pretty sure you will qualify."

Hard work. Focus. Dedication. Study. But also we need *vision*. What pulls us forward, and much of what is behind this book, is the future. Where is the church going? What will the future, the real future look like? The book of Revelation gives us the vision of a kingdom where Christ is the light of all of life and people from every nation or ethnic group are gathered around Jesus, and they are praising God and singing songs of thanksgiving and praise. In this book, I have tried to use such a vision, along with some of the best of what I have seen both in the history of the church and in my travels in the US, Africa, the Middle East, and Asia. So when you look back at some of the sections, or as you study chapters with your friends in your church, think of the description as the direction you should be moving in. The chapters intend to be hopeful, not judgmental.

GRACE IS KEY

When our boys were in high school we had an unusual gathering with their friends almost every Wednesday at a local restaurant at 6:30 in the morning. That is right. Adolescent boys, most all of whom were athletes in high school, made it to breakfast at 6:30 am. That means, of course that they got up before 6:30; sometimes about 6:25, but they were usually there. We would read a chapter of a Gospel or one from Galatians or Philippians, talk about what it meant for students in high school, and then pray and go off to school. We also told jokes. This went on for five years, until our youngest went off to college.

My greatest memories of those breakfasts (and it would happen about twice a year) occurred when we had deep conversations about relationships. Someone would talk about an important decision regarding a relationship with a teacher, a coach, or a parent (or girlfriend), and clearly there was no way forward if we expected justice. At that point I would say something like, "What is the hardest thing you will have to do in the world? Do you know? The hardest thing you will have to do is forgive."

> The hardest thing you will have to do is forgive.

That is right. Any relationship that will last—with friends, with parents, in marriage—requires you to forgive. No one is perfect and everyone will eventually offend you even if they don't want to. You will have to recognize this, step back, and just let go of your anger and your desire to get even. Forgiveness means that you dish out grace to others. It is really hard, but necessary.

The church is one of the supreme places to exhibit grace. As we get close to others, the masks that we wear and the personas that we project begin to slip and fall off. We realize that these leaders or brothers and sisters are not perfect. In fact, at times they seem very selfish. How can this be? We just studied about self-sacrifice and humility, and now Mary is asking for all the extra apple pie that is left from the dinner? We just talked about reconciliation in our community and Bob just told a racist joke. Really? We just spent thirty minutes at our church council meeting talking about the color of the curtains in the pastor's office? Really?

Our church, to become a place of healing and joy for others, must be a place of generous grace for its own. We don't just want to tolerate others in the church. We want positive forgiveness and dedicated prayer and support for those with whom we disagree. Such grace requires real faith that Jesus is the head of the church. It also requires patience with others. Faith and patience are ingredients of grace. In no way does this relieve us from speaking the truth if something bad is going on in the church, but we must cultivate faith that Jesus is really Lord of all (including our church) and patience to see things work out in God's good time.

We live in a time of instant satisfaction and impatience. So this may be hard.

HUMILITY IS THE ROAD

Ultimately, the local church is an institution dedicated to serving others. All that we have spoken about in the previous chapters builds on this simple truth. "He must become greater; I must become less" (Jn 3:30). In our *coming* to worship, we are turning away from our plans and our little world and stepping into God's great kingdom, accepting his plan for our lives. Thus, when we come we are coming to the cross and asking for God to crucify our little desires and raise up in our lives his great plan.

When we *stand* to praise, we are thanking God for who God is, and we are admitting our need for his acceptance and forgiveness. When we *kneel* we are confessing our sins and asking for forgiveness. We cannot do it on our own: we need Jesus to pay the price for our sins. When we *sit* to receive from God his refreshing word and life-giving body, we also are admitting again, in a different way, that we need what God has to offer. And finally, when we *go,* we go to empty ourselves for others; we are servants of the High King in mission. In all of these body movements that make up our worship and witness (chaps. 2 through 7) we are recognizing our need and our inadequacy.

Humility is the only proper stance or way to enter into his presence. We come on our knees, not with some kind of bravado or with our list of accomplishments. Humility makes worship powerful.

Humility makes fellowship in the church possible. Humility makes service to the children, the elderly, the needy, and the outsider both possible and genuine. As Jesus had the mind of humility (Phil 2:1-11), so we take on his mind and become his voice and his hands. The Church is, after all, the body of Christ *for the world*.

JESUS, THE MISSIONARY OF GOD, IS THE INSPIRATION

"As the Father has sent me, so I am sending you," Jesus said to his disciples as he prepared to depart to be with the father (Jn 20:21). We noted earlier that Jesus is the missionary of God and the church is the body of Jesus on earth. The church is a sent community that does not exist to simply protect us from the world but to prepare us to be salt and light in the world.

In fact, "The Church is the only society that exists for the benefit of those who are not its members."[1] That is right. Every week, every church needs to be aware of its worship, its basic discipleship, and pastoral care as being in devotion for the sake of its nonmembers. We want our children to grow into the likeness of Christ; we want our marriages, and all of our relationships, to reflect the humility and love of Christ, *for the sake of the nations*. Our ultimate concern is that God's glory be revealed to all of the world. The penultimate (next to the ultimate) goal is that the church be holy and wholly loving and gracious.

This should inspire every local congregation as it prays, plans, and then practices its faith. Are we growing in our witness to our community, to our friends and relatives, to our coworkers? Are we seeking ways to reach the unreached in this world? This should be the constant preoccupation of the leadership and the members of any local church. Jesus is our model as the missionary of God: he is our inspiration.

FINDING A CHURCH, PLANTING A CHURCH

People attend more than one church in their lives, and most of the people reading this book will move around to other churches for various reasons:

some good and some not so good. In my experience in different churches (I have moved around a lot) hardly any churches actually become heretical, but many make some pretty bad decisions that misrepresent the gospel of Jesus Christ. When thinking about where to become involved (not just attend) we should ask a few questions to keep us humble and honest.

1. Is there a place for me to serve *and* to learn and grow? Both are needed, and so we ask this as one question. If we can serve, but we are just getting burned out because the leadership does not provide ways to grow, then the church is not healthy, and it is easy to see that your time there will be short.

2. Is there a humble and well-informed leadership team? Not just the head pastor, priest, or bishop, but the team of people leading the church. If there is only one absolute leader (acting like a general or benevolent dictator) this is a problem. A good leadership team means there will be a group of people serving each other and serving the church. This is a healthy model for the church as a whole.

3. Does the church express, both in their worship and what they have recorded in print (on the website), beliefs and practices that are biblical and connected to the historic and global church in ways appropriate for the local community? Connection and context are important in any and every church.

4. Are their evidences of growth in humility and strength in community when you talk to people in the church? A few conversations in a small group or over lunch with some church members can tell you a lot.

5. Knowing that no church is perfect, is there at least some expression of the five body movements expressed in this book? It may be helpful to carry these concepts in the back of your mind when you visit and talk to people in the church.

Two final concerns I would like to bring up are *when to finish* and *when to start*. When, if ever, is it time to leave a church? We recognize that we live in a consumerist world, but when it comes to the church, we are not consumers, and the church is not a product. Therefore, the church is more like a family we are adopted into. So we commit to the people in the community, and these commitments are very important. Trust is built and churches are strengthened by the simple phrase, "I will love you folks anyway." The church is not the pastor, nor is the church the choir or the band leader or the worship leader, or any other individual. The church is something that Jesus died for, and so our commitment is serious and life giving. When anyone drops out because it is just too difficult, others will be hurt. We do need each other.

That is my strong statement on fidelity. Be faithful.

And yet, times come, as we all know, when a church has betrayed others, either by changing its doctrine or practices or by allowing obvious sinful practices to continue even when not condoning such practices. When this happens, we may have to talk to the leadership and eventually leave. I am quite aware of this because I am aware of the responsibility of parents when they take a child to church. A parent may be able to continue to serve faithfully in such an imperfect church, but for the sake of our children we may have to leave. I have expressed it this way:

> When we have children living at home, we go to church for the sake of our children. When the children grow up we go to church where we can best serve and have community.

I have been involved in churches that changed their theology or practices, and if these changes cut them off from their connections to Jesus and the church of history, it may be time to leave. Certainly, it is time to have discussions with your family and friends about what has happened.

Finally, what about starting a new church: church planting? To be brief, we need thousands of new churches planted today in the world, in virtually every community. We should never worry about there being too many churches in a city, or town, or too many college Christian groups on campuses. The work is too great and too precious to begin restricting new works. So many still have not heard the good news of Jesus Christ presented in a responsible way. We plant churches to reach the unreached, to love the unloved, and to invite in the lost. But we want to plant healthy churches that have a clear understanding of the calling of the Church.

We do not plant churches because we can't find a church that is just like us or me (that would be the wrong reason). However, we should be sending out from our local churches new church planting groups every few years. I can think of no good reason not to. If it is true that the Church is God's only plan for the redemption of the world, then we should do all we can for these redemptive communities to touch all of our neighborhoods. New churches should be planted from healthy existing churches. This book can be a guide for what a new church should look like. All of these new churches should see themselves as part of God's great plan (his kingdom), connected to churches through history and speaking to the local context.

NEVER-ENDING JOY IS THE RESULT!

As I finish the editing on this book, my wife and I are away on sabbatical for five months in a different state. We know only a few people in this city, and so we are once again doing some visiting around at different churches, learning about other churches, and trying to encourage some of the local leaders. As we did five years ago, we are visiting a variety of churches. One church we attended was a fairly recently planted church— about six years old but with over 1,000 in attendance. They have four or five worship sites, and they hope to reach all of the major cities in New England. It is an audacious vision. However, the vision and rapid growth was not what impressed us today. Even the very loud music (with free ear plugs!) was not so impressive. What was impressive was their commitment to community shown in little church gatherings that meet every week. These groups study the Bible and apply what they have heard from Sunday's sermon. Hundreds of people—diverse people from different ethnic groups, social classes, age groups—attend these groups, working every week at *doing* what the Bible says. This, according to Jesus, means they are building upon solid rock (Mt 7:24).

We were also impressed with the testimonies from the website. A very diverse group of people joyously gave testimonies of how the church had cared for them when a husband was dying of cancer, when someone was without work, and when they realized how much the church had given to help feed the poor in certain countries. It was interesting that each of the testimonies had some dark moments with suffering, but the overwhelming message was one of joy.

That is the way the church is. It is the place of genuine life, where we find what we were made for and how we can be what we were meant to be. That person we are becoming is connected to the Lord of life who gives us fullness of joy. We abide in the one who is Joy.

> I have told you this so that my joy may be in you and that your joy may be complete. (Jn 15:11)

NOTES

1 CHURCH: ONLY TWO PURPOSES

[1]Eucharist is often called the Lord's Supper or Communion (see Mt 26:26-28; Mk 14:17-24; Lk 22:17-20; and 1 Cor 11:23-26).

[2]I discuss Christendom in the next chapter. Defined briefly for now, it refers to the era when the Christian religion and Western political structures mutually supported each other.

[3]Christian witness involves pointing to Jesus with our life and our words. Christians are witnesses to his life and resurrection power.

[4]Kneeling or even going down on the ground in a prostate position signifies confession: confessing God's greatness and fullness and, thus, our emptiness. Even kings would kneel in the presence of the King of heaven and earth (2 Chron 6:13).

[5]Based upon work Dale Irvin and I did for the *History of the World Christian Movement* volumes (Maryknoll, NY: Orbis, 2001, 2012) and my recent book *The Unexpected Christian Century* (Grand Rapids: Baker Academic, 2015).

2 HOW DID WE GET HERE? FROM THE JESUS MOVEMENT, TO CHRISTENDOM, TO POST-CHRISTENDOM

[1]My attempt to explain that unity through time and all of geography is found in *Explorations in Asian Christianity: History, Theology, and Mission* (Downers Grove, IL: IVP Academic, 2017). My description of what holds Christianity together (coherence) is found on p. 150. Andrew Walls's description is given on p. 149.

[2]Baptism was used in the ancient world as an inauguration into a community. John the Baptist prepared the way for receiving Jesus' message by baptizing people in the Jordan River. Those who decided to follow Jesus and his teachings were to mark this new beginning by being baptized. See Mt 28:19; Acts 2:38; Rom 6:3; Gal 3:27-28.

[3]*Sacramentum*, in Latin, means "mystery." The mystery has to do with the presence of God in these acts and how grace is transferred through these acts. A sacrament is a holy mystery of God.

[4]For example, in John 1, Jesus is described as the Word of God. Does this mean a literal word (five letters of Jesus) or does it carry the complex meaning of the Greek word *logos*, translated "word"? If so, then Jesus is the meaning, the rationale, the

essence of God. How do you translate all of that into Syriac, Arabic, Gothic, and (eventually) English?

[5]Not actually written by the apostles, but reflecting the tradition of the apostles, its origins most likely lie in baptismal formulas or confessions before baptism. The earliest recorded edition dates from the late fourth century.

[6]This phrase "descended to the dead" or to Hades was added later, as an elaboration on how really dead Jesus was. See, among others, the classic discussion by Philip Schaff in *The Creeds of Christendom,* vol. 2: *The Greek and Latin Creeds with Translations* (New York: Harper & Brothers, 1877, 1919), 45-55.

[7]Translation by Alister McGrath in *"I Believe" Exploring the Apostles' Creed* (Downers Grove, IL: InterVarsity Press, 1991, 1997).

[8]The word *catholic* basically means the universal, or the whole, unified Church. It comes from the Greek word that means "according to the whole."

[9]Arius was an early fourth-century presbyter in North Africa.

[10]For a discussion of this controversy, see Dale T. Irvin and Scott W. Sunquist, *History of the World Christian Movement* (Maryknoll, NY: Orbis, 2001), 1:173-83.

[11]From the Nicene Creed, Philip Schaff's translation, in *Creeds of Christendom,* 2:58.

[12]"The impious Galilaeans (followers of Jesus) support not only their own poor but ours as well, all men see that our people lack aid from us!" From a letter from Roman Emperor Julian the Apostate to Arsacius, High Priest of Galatia, in *The Works of the Emperor Julian,* volume 3, Loeb Classical Library, translated by Wilmer C. Wright (Cambridge, MA: Harvard University Press, 1914), 71.

[13]A very early defense of Christian faith, written by Athenagoras ("A Plea Regarding Christians," dated about 177) explains this as common knowledge, "In your Empire, Your Most Excellent Majesties, different peoples observe different laws and customs; and no one is hindered by law or fear of punishment from devotion to his ancestral ways, even if they are ridiculous. A citizen of Troy calls Hector a god, and worships Helen, taking her for Adrasteia. The Lacedaemonian venerates Agamemnon as Zeus. . . . Among every nation and people, men perform whatever sacrifices and mysteries they wish. The Egyptians reckon among their gods even cats, crocodiles, serpents, asps, and dogs." Christians, however, claimed that Jesus was the universal savior for all peoples. In Cyril C. Richardson, ed., *Early Christian Fathers* (New York: Collier, 1970), 300-301; also available in the Christian Classics Ethereal Library (CCEL): www.ccel.org/ccel/richardson/fathers/Page_300.html.

[14]"Letter to Diognetus," chap. 5 in Richardson, *Early Christian Fathers*, 216-17; CCEL www.ccel.org/ccel/richardson/fathers.x.i.ii.html.

[15]"Letter to Diognetus," 217.

[16]Newbigin was a Presbyterian pastor, missionary, and bishop of the Church of South India. See *The Gospel and Pluralism Today: Reassessing Lesslie Newbigin in the 21st Century,* ed. Scott W. Sunquist and Amos Yong (Grand Rapids: Baker Academic, 2015).

[17]Paraphrased from a profound little article by Newbigin entitled "The Church: A Bunch of Escaped Convicts," *Reform* 6 (June 1990): 6.

[18]Constantine's conversion has been discussed extensively, but most agree that he certainly changed his mind and policies. See Peter J. Leithart, *Defending Constantine: The Twilight of an Empire and the Dawn of Christendom* (Downers Grove, IL: IVP Academic, 2010), 68-96.

[19]Recorded and transcribed from "The Crown," season 1, episode 4 (January 15, 2017), produced by Netflix.

3 COME

[1]John Bunyan, *Pilgrim's Progress*, chap. 3.

[2]*Liturgy* literally means "work of the people" or "public service." In the church it means the order of worship in a service, which includes readings, prayers, music, and preaching. In some churches the liturgy is more specific and detailed, in others it is less detailed and more open. Most liturgies point back to early patterns of worship in the Bible. The following chapters will discuss this more.

[3]From the Anglican *Book of Common Prayer*. When children are baptized, the parent(s) or guardian is asked, "Do you, in the name of this child, renounce . . . ?"

[4]St. Diadochos of Photiki, "On Spiritual Knowledge and Discrimination: 100 Texts," in *The Philokalia*, ed. and trans. G. E. H. Palmer, Philip Sherrard, and Kallistos Ware (New York: Faber & Faber, 1979), 1:288.

[5]John Eudes (1601–1680), "The Life and Kingdom of Jesus in Christian Souls," in *Bérulle and the French School*, trans. Lowell M. Glendon, S. S. (New York: Paulist, 1989), 293-94.

[6]I realize that I have moved from the phrase post-Christendom to non-Christian. I have done this deliberately because it seems that Europe and North America are becoming non-Christian in attitude and approach. Therefore, basic Christian principles like sabbath keeping and fidelity in marriage have become signposts for non-Christian culture.

[7]If you are not sure what Scripture calls sin, start with the Ten Commandments (Ex 20:3-17) and then look at Jesus' standards regarding the Law (Mt 5–7). Finally, there are "sin lists" in the New Testament (Gal 5:19-21; Col 3:5-11).

[8]The Greek word for church simply means "assembly," not building.

[9]Traditional Chinese have a Confucianist orientation to life, a daily concern for the ancestors, and may seek direction or make decisions according to the *feng shui*, astrological charts, or devotion they give at a Buddhist or Taoist temple. In a given family some members may frequent a Taoist temple, others a Buddhist temple. Devotion to the ancestors may take place at home or in a particular temple.

[10]Timothy Shultz, *Disciple Making among Hindus: Making Authentic Relationships Grow* (Pasadena, CA: William Carey Library, 2016), 42-52.

[11]Schultz, *Disciple Making among Hindus*, 49.

[12]I use the words *mission* and *witness* here interchangeably because God's command to make disciples (Mt 28) is parallel to his command to be his witnesses (Acts 1:8). Both are broadly inclusive terms. For a more thorough definition of mission see my *Understanding Christian Mission: Participation in Suffering and Glory* (Grand Rapids: Baker Academic, 2013), 173-74.

[13]Mark the Ascetic, "Letter to Nicolas the Solitary," in *The Philokalia*, 1:148.

[14]"Come, Now Is the Time to Worship," Brian Doerksen (Vineyard Songs, 1998).

4 STAND

[1]"Great Is Thy Faithfulness," by Thomas Obadiah Chisholm, 1923. There are many other praise hymns of this genre, such as "Immortal, Invisible, God Only Wise," by Walter Chalmers Smith, 1867.

[2]"Holy Is the Lord," by Chris Tomlin, on *Arriving* [CD] (Sparrow, 2004). Many Hillsong pieces would fit into this category. See, for example, "How Great Is Our God."

[3]Supplication is asking or begging for something.

[4]"I Can Only Imagine," written by Bart Millard; recorded by MercyMe (INO, 2001).

[5]"Revelation Song," by Jennie Lee Riddle, recorded by Phillips, Craig and Dean on *Fearless* (INO, 2009).

[6]I appreciate Edith Humphrey for first bringing this to my attention: *Ecstasy and Intimacy: When the Holy Spirit Meets the Human Spirit* (Grand Rapids: Eerdmans, 2006).

[7]*Hananim* is one of the main Korean words for God ("one" "Lord").

[8]Kim, Hwasik 김화식."김종섭 목사 약전 Kim Chongsŏp moksa yakchŏn" [A Short Biography of Rev. Kim Chongsŏp], *Sinang Segye* (June 1940): 22-37.

[9]Also known as African initiated churches or African indigenous churches, these African churches are not connected to Western churches but have their own origins in Africa.

5 KNEEL

[1]Worship is much more than singing songs of praise, but often it is reduced to that in newer worship communities.

[2]The NIV translation is actually "forgive us our debts, as we also have forgiven our debtors." Various forms of this prayer use "sins" instead of "debts," or "forgive us our trespasses as we forgive those who have trespassed against us."

[3]Contrition is an attitude of remorse or deep sorrow for sin, for what offends God. Psalm 51 expresses this attitude, which is the proper way to approach God, as a prayer: "The sacrifices of [or for] God are a broken spirit; a broken and contrite heart, O God, you will not despise" (Ps 51:17 ESV). I think it is helpful to see contrition, or a contrite heart, as healthy humility before God.

[4]See, for example, 1 Samuel 12. Deuteronomy 30 gives the warning to remind them to be faithful. Psalms 105–107 retell some of this history, focusing on God's faithfulness, even when Israel sinned. The "cry to the Lord" in these Psalms signifies confession and repentance, for it means they have given up on taking their own path and they are coming back to God and seeking his forgiveness and help.

6 SIT

[1]Six hours after writing this paragraph I came across an article in the *Religious News Service* titled "'Shocking' News on Worship and the Public" (May 3, 2017). The "shocking" news is that churchgoers are more interested in good preaching than good music. Preaching still is what attracts people to a particular church.

[2]I am aware that moveable type was used in China beginning around 1040 and in Korea soon after that. And I realize that metal moveable type was used in Europe in the fifteenth century. However, those earliest forms of moveable type did not yet cause a revolution in the availability of books for people. The Reformation in the sixteenth century was very much a movement fueled by printed booklets and sermons. Bible distribution for the laity was still slow in coming.

[3]In Orthodox, Roman Catholic, and Anglican churches, the confession comes after the sermon and reciting the creed.

[4]A helpful introduction to the use of the Christian year cycle is Bobby Gross, *Living the Christian Year: Time to Inhabit the Story of God* (Downers Grove, IL: InterVarsity Press, 2009).

[5]I am guessing that someone writing about "defects" in the clergy was not well received at gatherings of pastors. Today we try to express ourselves more positively: "Areas of growth for pastors."

[6]*Pia Desideria,* trans. Theodore G. Tabbert (Philadelphia: Fortress, 1964), 115. I replaced Spener's "men" with "folks."

[7]In many traditions we come forward to receive the body of Christ, some standing and others kneeling. We are using seated simply to symbolize that Jesus gives and we receive. We have done nothing; we sit (or come forward and kneel) with hands opened to receive from God.

[8]A sacrament is defined variously as an outward sign of an inward grace, or as something Jesus initiated and commanded us to do. Both baptism and the Lord's Supper are recognized by most Christians in the world as sacraments. Jesus submitted to baptism and commanded us to preach and baptize. Jesus initiated the communion meal and commanded us to do it to remember him. The Roman Catholic Church also includes five other sacraments along with these two: penance, anointing of the sick, confirmation, marriage or ordination to the priesthood, and extreme unction.

[9]"Good news" in Greek is *euangelion,* from which we get the word *evangelism*: to proclaim (*angel*) good (*eu*) news.

[10]We do not want to make this a point of contention, but most churches in the world do celebrate each week or at each gathering of the whole church. At a minimum a local congregation should be recentered on the suffering and glorious Christ through the Lord's Supper each month. Each local congregation or each network or denomination, if they are not committed to weekly remembrance, should be clear why they are *not* celebrating each week as the climax of the worship service.

[11]Most churches require membership or evidence (testimony) of being baptized in the triune name of God: Father, Son, and Holy Spirit.

[12]However, I will say that it would be good for all Christians to admit that God seems to have blessed churches that only baptize (or almost only) infants and those who only baptize adults who have professed their faith publically. Little is accomplished by arguing that all Baptists or Roman Catholics/Anglicans have disobeyed Jesus because of their practice of baptism through the centuries.

[13]From the word for *overseer* we get the word *bishop* (*episkopos*). As Paul traveled around the Mediterranean world he saw the need to ensure the consistent teachings and practices of the Church through appointed overseers who were entrusted with the correct teachings and practices.

[14]In fact, in many church traditions (Roman Catholic, Anglican) any baptized believer can baptize others. Our concern here is to make sure that the sacraments remain part of the church and not a private affair.

7 GO

[1]This term has the same source as the word *culture.*

[2]Richard Peace, *Holy Conversation: Talking about God in Everyday Life* (Downers Grove, IL: InterVarsity Press, 2006).

[3]Grand Rapids: Baker Academic, 2013. See pp. 297-99. In this first presentation of body movements for the church, I started with "stand" rather than "come."

[4]Oral English, oral Mandarin, Chinese sign language (ZGS), and Chinese writing in simplified characters.

[5]David Barrett, Todd M. Johnson, and George Kurian, eds., *World Christianity Encyclopedia*, 2nd ed. (Oxford: Oxford University Press, 2001), 656.

[6]It is interesting to note that both the Psalms and Proverbs focus on the life of the righteous and the wicked. The righteous live lives that make possible human flourishing and justice. However, not all people will be pleased with a new church in a community that promotes righteousness. Thus, Jesus and his body (the church) will not be universally hailed. Both Jesus and Paul promise suffering as we follow Jesus into the world.

[7]See Darrell L. Guder, "Missional Church: From Sending to Being Sent," chap. 1 in *Missional Church: A Vision for the Sending of the Church in North America*, ed. Darrell L. Guder (Grand Rapids: Eerdmans, 1998), 1-17.

[8]Rebecca Manley Pippert, *Out of the Salt Shaker and Into the World* (Downers Grove, IL: InterVarsity Press, 1979).

[9]Don Everts, Doug Schaupp, and Val Gordon, *Breaking the Huddle: How Your Community Can Grow Its Witness* (Downers Grove, IL: InterVarsity Press, 2016).

[10]Sign over the chapel door at Mt. Alvernia Nunnery Chapel, Pittsburgh, Pennsylvania.

8 HEALTHY BODY MOVEMENT

[1]"How Can I Keep from Singing?" aka "My Life Flows On in Endless Song," by Robert Wadsworth Lowery.

[2]New York: Macmillan, 1953.

[3]I have written about this question more extensively in chapter 7 of *Understanding Christian Mission: Participation in Suffering and Glory* (Grand Rapids: Baker Academic, 2013).

[4]This term was first coined by Ralph Winter of Fuller Theological Seminary in 1973 in Seoul, Korea, at the All Asia Mission Consultation. See chap. 19 in *Perspectives of the World Christian Movement* (Pasadena, CA: William Carey Library, 1981), 178.

[5]*ecclesiola in ecclesia.*

[6]See Kara E. Powell and Chap Clark, *Sticky Faith: Everyday Ideas to Build Lasting Faith in Your Kids* (Grand Rapids: Zondervan, 2011).

[7]John P. Bowen, ed., *The Missionary Letters of Vincent Donovan: 1957–1973* (Eugene, OR: Pickwick Publications, 2011), 83-93. See also Vincent Donovan's *Christianity Rediscovered,* 25th Anniversary Edition (Maryknoll, NY: Orbis, 2003).

[8]Still there were many divisions and sub-Christian movements that started. For a discussion of these divisions, see Dale T. Irvin and Scott W. Sunquist, *History of the World Christian Movement* (Maryknoll, NY: Orbis, 2001), 1:102-36, 155-94.

[9]English-language Bibles translate various words as *joy* or *rejoice*. In the King James Version the two words are found 377 times. In the NIV *rejoice* is found 154 times (192 times in the KJV), and *joy* is found in the NIV 218 times (185 in the KJV).

[10]Found in John Pollock, *George Whitefield and the Great Awakening* (London: Hodder and Stoughton, 1973), 118.

EPILOGUE: WHAT WE DID NOT TALK ABOUT

[1]Quotation from Archbishop William Temple, the head of the Anglican Church about seventy years ago.

SUBJECT INDEX

SCRIPTURE INDEX

EQUIPPING YOU TO PLANT
MISSIONAL CHURCHES

Fuller Seminary's Church Planting Program prepares men and women to plant and multiply missional churches. Our renowned faculty and experienced practitioners provide you with the healthy root system you'll need to plant a flourishing church that makes disciples and helps transform communities. We believe the three roots needed are (1) a biblical theology of church planting, (2) the spiritual formation of the planter, and (3) the missional skills to reach a post-Christian culture.

Outside the classroom, our apprenticeships, church planter student group, luncheons, and conferences introduce you to a variety of church planters and church planting networks to give you on-the-ground training for planting in a diverse, post-Christendom world.

LEARN MORE AT FULLER.EDU/CHURCHPLANTING
OR CHURCHPLANTING@FULLER.EDU.

Finding the Textbook You Need

The IVP Academic Textbook Selector
is an online tool for instantly finding the IVP books
suitable for over 250 courses across 24 disciplines.

ivpacademic.com